BERNI NEAL
ON LIFE, FAITH, AND LEADERSHIP

TEPEYAC LEADERSHIP SERIES

BERNI NEAL
ON LIFE, FAITH, AND LEADERSHIP

TEPEYAC LEADERSHIP SERIES

TLI
PUBLISHING
Phoenix, AZ

About the Tepeyac Leadership Series

Tepeyac Leadership, Inc. (TLI) is a nonprofit organization dedicated to civic leadership development for lay Catholic professionals worldwide. The Tepeyac Leadership Series aims to provide inspiration and insights for Catholics based on contemporary models of lay Catholic leadership. TLI offers a catalyst development experience that equips lay Catholics to become virtuous leaders, influence the culture and serve the common good. Learn more at TLIprogram.org.

The editor, Laurie Strom is a Deacon's wife, grandmother, and a former Executive VP & COO of SAE Industry Technologies Consortia and Honeywell Aerospace Director, where she managed engineering teams in multiple countries. Now, she is a mentor, coach, writer, and photographer - praising God and finding science and faith beautifully intertwined. There is beauty in a job well done.

Assistant Editor, Julie Bernhard, is a graduate of TLI 2025 Cohort. She currently works as a marketing executive, where she leads marketing strategy and execution for a corporate real estate firm. In her spare time, she enjoys cooking, shopping, and spending time with her family.

Cover Design: Maria Fernanda Hernandez

Copyright © 2025 by TLI Publishing
www.TLIprogram.org
Phoenix

Scripture verses contained herein are from the New American Bible Revised Edition, United States Conference of Catholic Bishops (https://bible.usccb.org/bible)

ISBN: 979-8-9907711-4-7

Printed in the United States of America

Dedication

This book is dedicated to the first eight cohorts of the TLI program -
2018 through 2025. May they continue to deepen their faith,
prosper in their professional pursuits, and become the virtuous
leaders they are meant to be.

"O Mother, strengthen the faith of our brothers and sisters in the
laity, so that in every field of social, professional, cultural and
political life, they may act in accordance with the truth and the law
brought by your son to mankind." (Pope St. John Paul II 1979)

Hail Mary
St. Juan Diego, Pray for us.

TABLE OF CONTENTS

(para. x) indicates the applicable paragraph number.

Page

Foreword   1

Introduction   5

Part 1 – Life   **6**

Immigrant experience – unique and rare (para. 1)   6

Heart for everything international (para. 7)   7

College, vocations and immigrant experience (para. 13)   8

Marriage? (para. 30)   11

Marketing skills and experience (para. 36)   12

Focus on family (para. 47)   14

Family and community leadership – early board service (para. 54)   16

Career mom (para. 71)   19

Most important – living truth (para. 89)   22

Photos   26

TABLE OF CONTENTS (CONT.)

(para. x) indicates the applicable paragraph number.

	Page
Part 2 – Faith	**28**
Earliest faith formation memories (para. 99)	28
Developing and deepening faith (para. 111)	30
Managing moments of doubting the faith (para. 115)	31
Responding to life challenges (para. 122)	32
Favorite prayers and saints (para. 127)	33
Collaboration with priests (para. 134)	35
Fear and humility (para. 135)	35
Litany of Humility	39

TABLE OF CONTENTS (CONT.)

(para. x) indicates the applicable paragraph number.

Page

Part 3 – Leadership   **40**

Board service - selection (para. 141)   40

Board service - experiences (para. 147)   41

Board responsibilities and the widow's mite (para. 149)   42

Board planning (para. 155)   44

Advice for future leaders - TLI (para. 159)   45

Where are lay leaders needed the most? (para. 162)   46

Being Catholic in a secular world (para. 170)   48

Faith and leadership in the family (para. 176)   50

European faith and culture experience for children (para. 180)   51

Catholic definition of success (para. 191)   53

Appendix I - The Power of Philanthropy   57

Appendix II - God's Call, A Woman's Response   69

Appendix III - Quotations and Scripture: Writings on the Walls   75

FOREWORD

Power, Charm, Grit and Faith

It only took until the pasta course for both Cardinals and several bishops to take a quick liking to my mother. We were in Rome at a dinner with an impressive roster of clergy and lay people, and still the room seemed to swing with a magnetic force towards Berni Neal. "I think your mom might come out of her shell one of these days", a Cardinal joked. She was persuading them to start a Twitter account for the College of Cardinals. It was 2008 and Twitter was in its relative infancy. My mom is always on the forefront, delivering her lightning bolt ideas with so much grace and warmth that they suddenly seem doable.

Berni is a force. She is a connector, a trusted mentor to many, a faithful Catholic, a genius marketer, a brilliant nonprofit thought leader, and a humble Orange County housewife and grandmother. Her endless creativity, no option left unexplored, translates to big solutions for boards and three granddaughters who are constantly inspired and charmed by their grandmother. Their play sessions can include a role-playing restaurant, hula dancing, spice tasting, book writing, a daily mass, and a trampoline picnic. And that's just one morning!

She brings this wave of creativity, energy, joy, and faith to everything she does. I worked for a restaurant group known in part for its cool factor, and Berni endeavored to host a beer launch party there for Benedictine monks. It was the first time the staff had met a monk, let alone seen one in person, and it was one of the best nights of the year.

My mom is not self-conscious. She is comfortable in her own skin wherever she goes. It's so disarming that people around her - strangers, friends, Cardinals, the neighborhood bakery owner - all take to her instantly. She stays in touch with the person who detailed our car once when we lived across the country.

I will always be grateful that my mom decided to leave paid work to be with my brother, Collin, and me. I watched in awe as she walked away from her ultra glamorous career for us, and to gracefully

1

support my father and his work. Her parenting style and leadership style are one: she uses optimism, wonder, and restraint to bring out the best of everyone around her, leaning on the Virgin Mary as an example.

My mom wrote me this note when I was deep in my first postpartum season that allowed me to enjoy the highs and lows of new motherhood:
"I am the mother who was so blessed to be chosen to accompany you during your pilgrimage on Earth. Tour guide might be the best description. The Blessed Mother did not 'make' Jesus Christ a better, smarter, holier person. And, interestingly, she's considered the 'best mom ever' precisely because her humility and motherhood ensured that His gifts shone forth."

My mom is a profound example of how to help others shine. And she has a freight truck of momentum behind her, powered by the true, the good, and the beautiful. I'm grateful to have a front row seat to the dynamism that is Berni Neal and hope you will enjoy this peek into the power, charm, grit, and faith that is my mother.

Kira Potter
Daughter of Berni Neal

INTRODUCTION

How to be a layperson in the world is to be a Catholic who is joyful and proud of it. Just be so filled that you are given the ability to share the overflow. I'm grateful that, by God's grace, I have received the gift and opened the box. I just want others who are holding the box to open it up. (para. 175)

The Tepeyac Leadership Series aims to provide inspiration and insights for Catholics based on contemporary models of lay Catholic leadership. The objective of the book series and its intended focus is to showcase exemplary lay Catholic leaders. This book features Berni Neal, a Latina Asian from immigrant parents who forged her professional path in multicultural marketing, discerned the call to place family and faith at the heart of her vocation and became a prominent Catholic philanthropist.

In an engaging question-and-answer interview format between Berni and Laurie Strom, editor for TLI Publishing, Berni shares the wisdom gained from moments of trial, grace and everyday acts of presence and prayer. She models how authentic lay Catholic leadership, virtuous education and lifelong formation transforms families, parishes, and the world.

Berni Neal: on life, faith, and leadership is a celebration of courage, faith, and authenticity. It was born out of admiration and desire to inspire future generations through Berni's example.

The book is structured to give the reader an insight into three concrete areas: the life, faith, and leadership of Berni Neal. With the aid of the table of contents, readers may jump into the area or questions they want to learn about first and explore the rest at their own pace. The text remains true to the conversation with Berni, but some of the questions have been modified to provide a smoother transition between topics. All proceeds from the sale of the book go to funding the mission of Tepeyac Leadership, Inc. (TLI).

Thank you for your interest in the life of Berni, your support of TLI, and the time you will dedicate to reading this book. We hope you find much inspiration in its pages to nurture your own life, faith, and leadership.

Part 1
Life

What's most important in life? Living in the truth. I try to be comfortable in my own skin - whatever gifts God has privileged me with, only for me in this combination, and my ability to stand before whoever the Lord presents; a stranger, and reach out to understand, "Why is this person in my life Lord? Why are we brought together to serve You?" - and not pretend to be somebody I am not. (para. 94)

1. Laurie: *Thank you, Berni, for being with us today to discuss life, faith, and leadership. You have an interesting cultural background and heritage. Please tell us about your family and where you grew up. Please take your time and just touch briefly on the most memorable moments of your early life.*

2. Berni: My parents are both immigrants. My father was born and raised in Cuba by Korean parents. My mother was born in the Dominican Republic; my French Spanish grandmother married a Chinese immigrant. My parents then met in California, who were Asian looking, but culturally, they were completely Caribbean Latino.

3. Then I was born in Orange County, California, home to strawberries, avocados, and orange groves. I was unique, if you will [being an Asian looking Latino]. In this setting, there were not many other cultures but it was a fabulous place to grow up. I grew up at home speaking Spanish and completely, culturally, Latina, Latina, Latina; food, music, friends, everything.

4. When I first met my husband, Rob, he was playing a cassette tape of music in the car. I said, "Wow, that's a really beautiful song. Who's that by?" He said, "You've never heard Bob Dylan?" I responded. "No, I've never heard this song before." He had no idea what to make of that.

5. I mean, beautifully for me, I was raised with my cousins as my friends, and my aunts and uncles as my sphere of reference. I'm going to call it my "immigrant experience," which was a very insulated world.

6. Now my family was mostly Methodist, and my mother was the Catholic. So, I had the beauty of being singled out yet again within my family. I'm the oldest of three children and I had to get ready for First Communion and Confirmation. My parents sent me to public school; I did not go to Catholic school. So not only, I'm thinking back, did I stand out within my public-school life, but then, even within the little community of my family, within that little space, I stood out because I was the Catholic kid. But I made the most of being unique and rare.

7. Laurie: *You mentioned your husband, Rob. How did you meet? Was that in college?*

8. Berni: Yes, we met in college at an organization that was an international club called AIESEC. The concept was that local chapters would generate internships and all the chapters around the world would do the same. Then all our names would be put into a hopper. My husband wanted to go to Japan; he hoped he would get matched with an internship in Japan, and then off he would go. Instead, Rob likes to joke that his lifelong internship has been being married to me, because being married to me is like being married to a global force. Neither of us ever went on an international internship through this organization, but that is how we met. We both had a heart for international business - international everything, but Rob at that time had never left the United States, and other than a trip to Hawaii, had never left California. So it was a very interesting first forty years of marriage!

9. Laurie: *Had you been out of the country when you went to college?*

10. Berni: Yes, because of my family. In the summers, my mom and dad would send me off to the Dominican Republic, and at Christmas as well. I loved it!

11. When I was thirteen, I asked my mom and dad if I could have the money they were saving up for my Quinceañera, my fifteenth birthday. It's like a sweet sixteen. I think it broke my mother's heart. I estimated that half of the funds could go towards my first car and the other half of the money would be for a trip to Spain organized by my Spanish teacher. The trip was during Easter week, and I wanted to see a procession. I'm appreciative that my parents were so bold and courageous. I was the firstborn, so they didn't have any idea of what was mature enough or not. So off I went to Easter Week in Spain!

12. This opened the door to other trips. When I was fifteen, I went to Easter Week in Mexico with my older Mexican cousins and friends. They let me tag along - another great thing I lived as part of the Latino culture. They didn't mind my being a younger cousin and raising my hand, "I want to go with you guys." They said, "Okay, come along," and off I went. They were all Mexican, and I was the American kid who tagged along. It was awesome!

13. Laurie: *That is fascinating. You were able to see and experience so much even before graduating from high school! Then you went to college. Was your background in college marketing?*

14. Berni: Yes. It was marketing. All of my friends were talking about going to college. I knew about it but had no idea how to embark on that process. My immigrant parents didn't have a connection to college, how to apply or arrange college tours. All of that was foreign. They whole-heartedly endorsed my attending college, but next steps were another story. My reach school was Berkeley. Truth be told, I wanted to apply to places that were far from home. The application fee was another hurdle. My mom and dad said, "Okay, let's find out what college is within a ten-mile radius of our home, and that's the one you get to go to." And so, as choices I had Goldenwest Community College and Cal State Long Beach. I attended Cal State.

15. Laurie: *With regards to your parents, what were they doing? What kind of vocation did they have?*

16. Berni: My dad arrived here [in California] with no English. He planned to study diplomacy and left for the US in 1957. Cuba was undergoing great turmoil with Fidel Castro challenging the Batista government. My grandparents sent him to Los Angeles where he had a sister who was a picture bride with a Korean man. That's another story. So, he became established in Los Angeles. He was able to live with my aunt, get a first job, and get a little bit of financial independence. During that time, he met my mother.

17. They married in 1960, and my dad did take a couple of trips back to Cuba. But by then, he had tasted American life and met my mother. My mother, by the way, was not accepted because she was not Korean, and she was mixed. She was half French Spanish. I don't think of it as racism because she was Asian - it wasn't that. There is always, I think, in human history that sense of, "you are other." You are not like me "enough." That was the case for my mom and dad, because my dad's siblings had married Koreans.

18. Laurie: *Wow, maybe that helped you then - their background of being other or being different? May that have helped them understand what it was like for you to be different from the culture?*

19. Berni: Absolutely, and it was my advantage when we had friends outside of my cousin circle who were Spanish speaking. My parents would meet others from all over - from Peru, Ecuador, Costa Rica; I had friends growing up whose parents were from many other Latin American countries.

20. Now, many of the children were not speaking Spanish. They were truly trying to become "American." My parents said, "No, absolutely not. You will have the benefit of being bilingual." Culturally, what they knew was Latino, so Spanish is what we spoke at home.

21. Looking back, I'm very grateful to my parents for emphasizing the beauty of the otherness, and yet the importance of sameness, because we're all people, you know. So, we throw down a chicken. Everyone made it in different ways. But okay, we've got chicken six different ways. This could be great, and it was! So yes, I credit my parents for having the love for their roots, of how they grew up culturally. It wasn't ethnic, it was cultural, and they surrounded me with that cultural stew. But I did see parents who said, "Nope, they are going to speak English." And those children spoke English.

22. Laurie: *What a gift! If your parents didn't have a background in college education, how did you decide that was a path you wanted to go on?*

23. Berni: There is a French philosopher, René Girard, who talks about mimetic desire - you just want to copy what other people are doing, and whatever's hot and cool and trendy. Honestly, that's what it was. Like all the other students in my junior year, I had to take the PSAT. "Okay, fine, whatever. What is that?" And you figure it out. I wasn't involved in after-school activities, but I caught out of the air a sense of what was happening. After school, I was home with my family, and then on weekends, I was with my cousins. All my cousins were going through the same sort of children-of-immigrants experience.

24. So, I have a great affinity and distinct memory of that challenge. I remember being in kindergarten and looking at the teacher and thinking, "Yeah, words are coming out. But what is going on?" My mom says I picked up English very quickly, which children do. But I have very, very powerful memories of that experience.

25. In the late sixties, early seventies my aunts, uncles and cousins started arriving in from Cuba. I remember sharing beds and sleeping bags, sharing clothes, everything - and the language, just that kind of stuttering that would happen. Culturally, they didn't like hot dogs. "Well, why don't you like hot dogs?" I mean, just as a child, trying to adjust to that. It was very powerful. I've heard people call it traumatic. I had the great blessing of no trauma - absolute richness. The language we use to describe it makes a difference. Sure, you can paint it as trauma, but what if we help somebody say, "But tell us, what was the fruit of that?"

26. I have that privilege, again, that my parents knew that the language and the culture would allow me to be richer, and they said to me, "You'll stand out." Some people could say, "Yeah, you'll be a freak!" But I said, "Well, being a freak seems to be a good thing in my parents' household. So, I'm good. I'm going to go with that." And it was really, truly so healthy.

27. Laurie: *How you frame things can make such a difference! So, how did you choose marketing as a college major then?*

28. Berni: Marketing came up because my household was middle class, but during those teenage years, the mimetic desire for what everyone else has - and now I want it, too - was strong. I may not need it, or it doesn't make sense, but I want it. I thought to myself, "Well, my whole life I've been persuading my dad that I need THIS; and I have to have THAT; the price point is worth it; this is a value proposition! Marketing is totally in my wheelhouse. Come on, it's a no-brainer. I'll coast through college!" I can half joke about it, but that really was the motivation. I considered majoring in economics. And I thought, "Economics? But marketing is the driver. It's the glamourous side of Econ. So I'll try that." Marketing is what I pursued.

29. When I said I was going to college, my dad said, "Yes, you are going to college." My grandfather, who migrated from Korea to Cuba, was literate, and that was rare in those days. (This was in the early nineteen hundreds.) Being immigrants to Cuba, they were the serfs; to be honest, they were the laborers. Because my grandfather was literate, it allowed him to be admin for the community. My grandfather died in Cuba the year after I was born; I never met him. So, education was important, and my dad told me I was going to college. But how to get there, my dad said, "That's your problem. You figure that out, and it's got to be within ten miles of our house."

30. Laurie: *Oh, a good problem-solving challenge! So, then you met Rob at college. How did that work? Did you have your career for a while, and then you got married, or what was that like?*

31. Berni: We were friends. We were in the college club, AIESEC, I mentioned earlier. Rob was the chapter president, and I was a club member. He asked me out on an official date. At the end of the evening, he asked, "So what do you think about marriage?" And I thought, "Gosh, this guy has nerve. I mean, we're friends, but I know this is a date. This isn't just the gang going out for a beer. But come on!" So, I said, "I really love the idea of marriage. I hope to be married one day, but it won't be to you. But you're really nice, and I hope we can go on other dates, but I won't be marrying you." Rob remembers it as I said. "I wouldn't ever marry **you**!" with emphasis. (I hope I was more polite about it.) But he said, "Really, why?" - like why wouldn't it be me? And I said, "Well, you're not Catholic."

32. And so that was date one. By date four, on his own, he went to RCIA [Rite of Christian Initiation of Adults], but I didn't find out about it. We started dating in September, and in December he said, "I want you to be my Confirmation witness." That's when he let me know he was going to go through this; he was converting. Then he asked me to marry him, and - there you go!

33. Laurie: *He was smitten right from the beginning!*

34. Berni: Well, we had been friends... I highly recommend that to the youth. It's hard to recommend that because the concept of dating and courtship and being friends is so foreign compared to what Rob and I experienced. I'm trying to learn more about what the youth are going through today. That's a whole societal conversation. But that's the way we did it. We were friends first because we were in a group. For youth today, I say, be a part of your Life Teen or your church groups, or in college, be a part of something, because, you know, sitting in your house gaming isn't going to do it!

35. So, Rob and I were married pretty much right after my college graduation. He graduated the year before me and had already started his career path in real estate in college. When I got out of college, I knew it was going to be marketing. I bounced around in different jobs until motherhood found me, which is really my vocation.

36. Laurie: *When you had those different jobs, you were quite successful in them in terms of learning marketing skills. You know what works. So how long was that - two or three years?*

37. Berni: I worked for about four years after graduation. I landed at an ad agency the year after we were married. I knew I was home, so to speak, professionally. We married in 1983, and our daughter was born in 1987. I continued to work, a working mom, because that's what you did back then. The attitude was "We can do it all!" Mommy Wars: working moms vs. stay-at-home moms was raging and looking back, I wish I would have chosen the other side. Do you remember that [1970-1980s] Enjoli commercial for perfume?

38. Laurie: *No...*

39. Berni: Okay, so it's worth bringing up because it's so ridiculous. It's a woman with this fabulous evening gown, beautiful, flowy, dreamy, and she's wielding a frying pan in the other hand because she can do everything, right? This is my profession at its successful worst, really selling the lifestyle and influencing the culture, through a perfume.

40. My advantage in advertising was, given my background, I understood the fact that every single customer in the United States has green money; whatever color they may be, their money is green, and my role was to present the fact that my client's product is worth opening their wallet for. I had an almost instinctual - which everybody has really, if you put it that way - everybody does understand - but I could get to the germ of what's going to make a human being want this product. When you get to that core truth, and then (unfortunately) use it to connect consumer and product, you are a winner; you win for your client. But it was just that ability to understand. Let's go to the core reason why a customer would want this product. Strip away all the other stuff. Now the retail, transactional conversation takes place.

41. Providentially, my role in the ad agency business was as a liaison between the agency and the client. My agency experiences exposed me to an incredible roster of clients: Pepsi, Honda, Nike, Kraft Foods, I was even involved with the launch of the California Lottery. I was exposed to so many different businesses. You must be more than proficient at your client's business to be able to speak about it intelligently to their consumer.

42. Because I had this background of already being from disparate cultures, you know, chicken cooked six different ways, I was already, just from birth, imbued with this idea of multiple things and then how to distill it down to its essence to understand what's important. So I was a shoo-in for advertising. And then I came of age at a time when the idea of "Oh, we have a critical mass of Spanish speakers in the United States." "Oh, lo and behold! You have this African American audience who has a cultural nuance that is different than the general market." (At the time it was insulting to say black. It was very politically incorrect to say black, but now we go back and forth between the two terms.) And then I looked Asian because I am Asian. We had a smaller population of Asians and how to reach them as a

consumer was not as dramatic as the Spanish-speaking, or the Ebonic-speaking (which was the accepted term at the time at a multi-cultural agency to identify this cultural group beyond color). Really, I came of age at the right time given my cultural heritage.

43. The Muse *Cordero Chen agency* had cohesively put that together and said, "Okay, we're going to think about advertising to these audiences in a very universal but specific way." So again, my background, my look - I mean, I was tailor-made for that time. I had a great time meeting and talking to people at my client meetings.

44. I remember one client meeting with a home savings bank - huge. I think it was *Home Savings and Loan* - very proper banking. I had to go through what felt like four or five layers of receptionists to get to what looked like a vault door, and when it opened, it was this huge conference room. I said things that were politically incorrect and breaking barriers in the space. I had to break through and say, "You know who else has savings accounts? These families are not customers you are accustomed to. So, let's talk about what they're doing and why they're saving. How their child is the one who speaks English, but the parent doesn't. But the parent has the power of the purse, and the child has the power of interpretation." I was more of an ambassador; I could speak from the heart.

45. Laurie: *Yes, I see you were providing very early on that idea of Both/ And, right?*

46. Berni: Yes, very early on the power of that Both/ And! Because Either/ Or - someone is going to lose with an Either/ Or, but with Both/ And - Woohoo! We've just upped the number of guests at the party. Wonderful!

47. Laurie: *That's awesome. So, what made you decide to step out of that high-powered kind of world and focus on the family?*

48. Berni: At the time, because *AT&T* was one of my clients, I was traveling almost every week. I would try to do a quick trip up to Washington State and then fly back. I once flew to San Francisco twice in one day for Hills Bros Coffee. It was crazy. My husband, Rob, was in commercial real estate, and was also flying all over the country. Rob and I had a sit-down and said, "Okay, this is not right.

Our marriage is job one, but in our ability to raise our children, which is our job 1.5 (I won't reduce it to two) ~ we are failing."

49. We put our careers as number one, and then our marriage as catches as catch can. And then... are the children fed? Are they clean? But they're not pets! So that is what put us in the position of being serious about one of us needing to stay home and be with our children. We are their formation. How are they being educated and who are their teachers?

50. We had wonderful nannies who helped us along the way. At one point, we tried to blend that by bringing my aunt to live with us. She was a single woman and had lived in New York. We said, "Okay, at least, if it's a family member, that will definitely be many steps above," and it was great, but it still wasn't us.

51. We felt we had to take more responsibility for them. And it was tough. I had made it to vice president. I had been invited to become a partner, and it was a done deal. That was kind of a fork in the road, and it forced Rob and me to quit talking about it and to make a decision. Frankly, we waited too long to make a decision. I'm grateful that the agency invited me to become a partner because it made me seriously examine our priorities. There was a great temptation to accept the new role and responsibilities. I would have professionally arrived, you know?

52. VP and partner, and all of the perks that came with that dangled in front of me but through the gifts of the Holy Spirit, prayer and discernment, Rob and I had to say, "Okay, look at these cherubic" ~ well, at that point they weren't so cherubic, but ~ "look at these two faces here, and then all that the world can give you." As tempting as that was, I knew that the choice had to be the children. Rob and I joke, and we don't really remember the moment, but I joke that we took a penny and flipped a coin as to whether it was going to be him or me that stayed home. I won the coin toss...

53. It was a difficult decision because I loved the client roster. I loved the team that had been built. I loved the vision of this agency, which was just so unique at that moment in time to speak to the different cultures and ethnicities. And it was another version of a civil rights

moment in a consumer sphere. It was a difficult decision, but it was absolutely the right decision.

54. Laurie: *I think that is a message that others struggling with similar choices may need to hear. You certainly seem filled with joy now, even though it was a difficult decision at the time. After that, I think you mentioned in your background that you went on to serve on a board?*

55. Berni: Well, I did both at the same time. So, now I'm an at-home mom and my children were at school for six hours a day. What am I going to do with myself? I don't play tennis. I don't golf. I eat lunch, but you know that really could become a problem (and it did)! So I showed up at the *Girl Scouts* Headquarters; I walked in and said, "You know I was a Girl Scout. I never got my gold pin, but I really loved the organization."

56. It meant so much for me to watch my mother in her leadership role. My mother came to the US when she was fourteen. By the time she was twenty-five, she was married with three children under five, and by thirty, she was a troop leader. I thought, "Wow! My mom's important. This is great!" It was so foundational for my ability to see myself as a mother and a leader to watch my mom take those roles.

57. One was being responsible for the cupcakes; when you're seven or eight, if your mom made the cupcakes, that's a big deal. My friends admired her because they were great. I say that because I want other moms and dads who hear this to know that those seemingly tiny moments are so important. It was to me; I get emotional even.

58. So I walked into the Girl Scout Office and - just to truly show you the Holy Spirit, the Minxy Holy Spirit - they said, "Oh, the executive director can meet with you if you have a moment." Well, I didn't know what an executive director was. I knew what a troop leader was. I knew these offices tabulated cookie sales, but I had no idea what went on there, because my world had been professional at a company, but I didn't know the nonprofit world. No correlation.

59. So I sat down and met with the executive director. She said to me, "I would like you to return and come to a board meeting to speak

about your experience as a Girl Scout." I did, and then, next thing I know, I'm nominated, and I'm on the board. I thought, "Okay, so what is a board like? I've heard of them; their pictures are all over the place. But what is a board?" And in a nonprofit space, it was even more of a curiosity to me. I was terrible at it. The *Girl Scouts* did not take time to explain the expectations and responsibilities; onboarding as it is referred to now. It is likely they assumed I knew.

60. I did not have the benefit of being in a sorority or in the Greek system. I've watched, and I've seen how important those sorority and Greek fraternity systems are to help people learn; people have positions of leadership and learn those sorts of things. I did not have that. I had to learn quickly, and I didn't do well. They did invite me to attend the National Conference, which was in Indianapolis that year, and that was an eye-opener. I was hurt because of what they were proposing at that time, the things that they wanted for girls and their vision going forward. I was not in alignment with GSA (Girl Scouts of America). Frankly, it was a painful thing, and I quickly said, "I don't recognize this organization, and if you're going that way, I'm going to fight you tooth and nail to go in another direction."

61. By now I was home, [not working professionally], and I was getting involved in a prayer group that was on campus for the children's school: praying for the children, for their holiness, formation and safety, and for the faculty, and so forth. Then I got into what would be the equivalent of a PTA and joined that board. When they found out I had abilities in marketing, it became a no-brainer: "Berni knows how to promote our things." But then, I'd talk about "What's our vision statement? What's our business plan?" and they thought, "Oh, this woman is intolerable!" Many of these women knew what those things were but thought, "We don't need to do that for our school." "Come on!" I said, "Yes, we do. We really do, because I won't know what to do if we don't have that roadmap." And so, it was really fun working with a lot of these women and getting to know the moms who did work and the moms who didn't work.

62. I tried to be a bridge because the moms who worked didn't have time for lengthy meetings. It was an interesting time emotionally to be in that hybrid space of the haves, as in those who have a job, and the have-nots, those who don't have a job. It was clear those were enemy

camps at that time. They were wary of each other. One looked down on the other.

63. Laurie: *Do you think that still exists a little bit?*

64. Berni: My interpretation is, it still exists but it is a way to justify what we're doing. If I'm a working mom, I may speak ill of the non-working mom, but I do it as a way to justify myself. Whereas before I would say there was a hostility: "You're college educated, and you can have a job, and you can be a VP and a partner. What do you mean 'No'? Your children will be fine."

65. Right now, it's more a sense of "I know this isn't right, but this is what I choose to do." This is anecdotal, but I've heard from enough young women who say, "Yes, our household income, as husband and wife, is enough for one of us to stay home, but we both choose to work because otherwise we just wouldn't be good mothers and fathers. We wouldn't be good human beings because we just couldn't stay home all day." And I listen, and I hear that, and I accept that, but I always want to speak more about it with them, because my experience was that I made a career out of being a mother. There's so much to being a mother that to be so cartoonish about it is really regrettable.

66. So first, I came home emotionally, and then I would pick up projects on the side because I had six hours a day to do whatever. I was starting to learn, to get on boards and such things.

67. Laurie: *At that time, were your children in a public school or a Catholic school?*

68. Berni: For those first five years, my children were in a public school, and we were trying to get into the Catholic school, but the parish had a lottery system. Then, in the middle of that, we moved to Denver, and then we came back. So with job changes and things over those five years, we never got into Catholic school; we were there at the wrong time, we moved at the wrong time, just things.

69. We made the decision; they're going to go to Catholic school, a private Catholic school, where we don't have to be a part of the parish (which didn't seem to be helping). So that's how we got them

into Catholic school. But for those years that they were in public school, I would pick up side projects.

70. So I didn't go cold turkey into full-time mom because my aunt was living with us. And I was kind of afraid of it in many ways. I just didn't know how to do it. I was so bombarded with this thing of you've got to work. You have to work - you can't just say you're a mom. What's on your business card? Do you even have a business card if you're a mom? It was those weird, stupid things. But there it was.

71. Laurie: *You mentioned making a career out of being a mom. Can you talk a little bit more about what that career is like? How does it benefit both the children and you from a fulfillment perspective?*

72. Berni: So I would go back to what I watched with my mom being a career mom. My mom was a full-time mom, but she volunteered. She was my teacher. She trained me in folding clothes, and all the other things that she wanted me to learn. She was my educator. Her career was a 360 on life.

73. When I took on the role, I was burdened with this idea that you had to do both. You had to have a professional career on a payroll outside of the home. Because you didn't have remote work options back then, you had to commute somewhere. If you got to travel, that was glamorous. Versus a full-time mom, which was the stereotype of all the reverse of that: You're tied. You're stuck. All of those very anchoring concepts, but with a negative connotation.

74. But for me, mom became a career. My children will tell you that if they wanted something, or were planning something, they had to put together a PowerPoint and present it to me. And then one time my son says, "Mom, I am not your employee! And please, please get a job!"

75. Laurie: *Probably thinking, "This was so much easier when you were working!"*

76. Berni: Yes, for them, so much easier. Oh, my gosh!

77. When I really came home and looked at motherhood as a career, my son was in third grade, and my daughter was in fifth grade. So they had enough years of me trying to be both, or whatever that was. I don't know that I did anything well, but look, they survived my early years of trying to figure out who Berni Neal was as a human being, wife and mother. I had to align those first two things, then everything else fell into place, and I was able to move fully into being the kind of wife and mother that I had the potential to be.

78. So, here's what I learned. I learned that being a full-time mom did not mean that I was not going to apply all my professional skills. Nonprofits really needed marketing services, and I could provide them in a non-transactional way. My performance evaluation? Frankly, if they kicked me out, fine; I was free anyway. It gave me great liberty just to be honest with these organizations because I wasn't having to worry about being liked or not liked, or whatever. I was giving my time because I loved the organization, and whether they loved me or not was not the point. I hoped that we could collaborate and do well because the mission became the main thing.

79. With my children, it was kind of the same thing, because what was my agenda? It was not to have them make me look good if they got 100% on their spelling bee. It wasn't a reflection on me. It was their spelling bee. That was also a very key driver for me. I was not going to come home and be an at-home mom to spend three hours after school doing their homework with them. I wouldn't do that with somebody on my professional team. I wouldn't handhold them that way. Why would I do that with my child?

80. I had friends who said, "Oh, my gosh! Last night I spent xx hours on..." whatever the project all the children were working on. I tried to be mindful of how I worded it, but I asked, "Is that your child's project? How are they going to learn if you've done it for them?"

81. So as a career mom, I turned birthday parties into goodwill events, not unlike corporate outreach events for clients. Consumer live events was a growing niche because you wanted the consumer to experience your product. So, that's what I did: all of these different things that my children were involved in, or that the school or the nonprofit wanted to do - no problem! It just became an extension of whatever I had learned and whatever skills I did have at that point to

apply them here. Being a mom does not eliminate the different activities that you learned to do professionally. You're not on payroll but you are rewarded.

82. Laurie: *So let's talk about that. Talk about it from your children's perspective, from your perspective, and from Rob's perspective, the fruit of the decision you made to be at home.*

83. Berni: Yes. Well, it would be great to ask my children that question, and they probably would love to answer it. I won't speak for them other than to say there were times when they would say, "Could you please just get a real job and travel again, because that would be so helpful." But for me, I was just free from expectations of performance that were legitimate in the business world, like, "Are you hitting your numbers? Are the clients' contracts growing? Are they firing us?" I get it, but children do the same thing. If your child tells you, "I am not fixing my bed," that is my deliverable. I have to figure out a way to get my child to feel that it is an important responsibility he has, and he's going to do it. I know that's almost banal, but it is applicable. It is the same thing. The desired outcome is the same ~ a result. But how I felt about it was that mind shift of ~ this is important. My child's ability to feel that participating in a household doing laundry together, folding clothes together, whatever, is important.

84. At the time, we lived in a condo; it was a small condo, which is funny, but the location was amazing. This is where I wanted to live. Rob said, "I really want to build a house." I said, "Okay, that's great. How long is that going to take?" He said, "Well, about three years: Find a lot, find the architects and build the house." I said, "Fine for three years, can I pick where we live?" He said, "Yes."

85. I thought, "Where do the tourists go when they vacation in Southern California?" I found a beautiful little condo building on the water in Newport Harbor, and we had a blast. It was great because as a family we were on top of each other. We grew together because here in California, and I would assume many places in the United States, there is this presumption that each family member should have a lot of space and have a great deal of privacy. Well, we had a condo, and we were going to make it work.

86. I said to the family, "Think of this as a bigger hotel room with a kitchen and a coin-operated laundry downstairs." We needed a lot of quarters to do laundry, and we had to juggle laundry schedules with the other condo owners. It was hilarious. But wow, it forced a whole other sense of respect and teamwork. My children were glad to move into a dorm because they had suites and housekeeping!

87. Laurie: *What a great learning experience and what great memories!*

88. Berni: I don't know if I'm answering all your questions, Laurie, but I'm having a great time telling you these stories!

89. Laurie: *Well, I think that is important! One of the key elements we hope to share is what is important in life when you look back at it. What have you found most meaningful from that perspective? You clearly have enjoyed life. And so, when you look back at it, what would you share with others about what's most important in life?*

90. Berni: I think, living in that truth of what is important. When I asked myself, is achieving partnership, winning awards, increasing market share for my clients more important compared to my daughter having a slumber party? And you know it would be an all-nighter, cooking all night, and just being present. I'm not one of the girls, but being present... that time is just invaluable. That is important.

91. But also, from a spiritual sense. We speak of the moment of Christ's crucifixion as being both in the Kairos and the Chronos. In our human Chronos, it was at a point in time, but in the Kairos, we were all there, in that moment. So, in some ways, being present in those little moments of my children's lives as they grew up is Chronos and Kairos because they carry that forever. Vital. So, when I string together the pearl necklace of memories, I'm so glad because those moments were just so meaningful.

92. Now, there were also moments where I'd say, "I could have been at a really cool pop-up party in New York after work with my clients," which was the last thing I did in my professional career. It was interesting timing from the perspective of temptation. There was a pop-up; a celebrity was throwing an event at a secret location. They

had called one of my friends and we were going to show up there in a limousine. I'd started the day at a NY salon after getting off a red-eye to prep for a client meeting. I mean all that stuff. It was my "last hurrah!" before changing over to full-time mom. I could throw away my business cards, because that was it. You see what the tempter is up to? Because "Wow, this is so exclusive, and I can tell all my friends about it." But I thought, "What is IT? IT is so fleeting. So terribly unimportant and frankly, superficial in the doing and in the telling!"

93. But I was keenly aware of the stark contrast and terribly unglamorous side of motherhood. Even the dreariest parts of working seem important (reviewing billing, client memos [emails], admin, etc.) as compared to another load of laundry, grocery shopping, and carpooling.

94. So, again what's most important in life? Living in the truth. I try to be comfortable in my own skin - whatever gifts God has privileged me with, only for me in this combination, and my ability to stand before whoever the Lord presents; a stranger, and reach out to understand, "Why is this person in my life Lord? Why are we brought together to serve You?" - and not pretend to be somebody I am not.

95. My husband Rob loves cars. When the children and I grew out of our minivan, I was crushed because I really loved that van. Rob said, "You don't need a minivan. Really, you don't need a minivan." So I've "labored" under the fancy cars that he thinks I've needed all these years. Rob finally came to accept, "She really wants a minivan. Why am I fighting her?" So, I am now the proud owner of a new minivan! But post-galas, when everyone is lined up waiting for hotel valets to bring forward the cars, Rob's car inevitably arrives first. He is such a gentleman that he waits with me, and we get to further socialize until my car arrives. It was all fine until one of his buddies called out the disparity in our cars. So it's a silly thing, but it's a material example of trying to be comfortable in my own skin even though friends poke fun and Rob good-naturedly endures it.

96. During a college heart to heart with my daughter, I told her, "When I gave birth to you, the Lord entrusted to me your hourglass." I said, "It is your sand. How you spend your sand is your business. I'm here to make sure the hourglass doesn't get broken, and that you

place your hourglass in good, safe, humble and worthwhile places, but that's your sand."

97. Also, there is the importance of detaching myself and not being a helicopter mom. Are their lives a reflection on me? Yes, but those are choices she makes, and my son makes. I have to live in my own skin and walk in my own relationship with our Lord. Our Lady had the suffering of watching what others did to her son. What does the Lord ask me to do? What has He spoken so clearly to me? How do I make sure that I'm responding to His call? If my children don't do what would make me look good as a mom because they did LMNOP instead, so be it. Would it make me sad if they did things that were illegal or hurtful to someone else? Yes, but as my parents taught me, "You're going to speak Spanish, whether it's cool or not cool. You know you're going to be the only Spanish-Asian kid in a classroom full of others. Navigate it. Own it." That is me, and my children are related to me, but they have their own successes and failures.

98. That would be the other thing I would say to moms is to walk tall and proud and confident if you are responding to the Lord's call. Your children's successes are things to be proud of, but their failures are not yours. Their successes are not yours either. They are proud moments. Do not get so wrapped up in them. They've got to grow up to be their own people. It is their hourglass and their sand.

Life

26

Church of Santa Maria Della Vitoria, Rome, Italy
Faith

St. Juan Diego Leadership for the World Award
With Bishop Olmsted and Cristofer Pereyra
Leadership

Part 2

Faith

Trusting in God's Chronos, because we have Kairos. We don't live in Kairos, but we have Kairos because in the moment that the Lord was crucified, offered up His soul and descended into hell - in that moment - everything was there, past, present, and future. (para. 118)

---

99. Laurie: *Berni, from our discussion on life, it is clear that your faith is a very important foundation for your decision making. We would like to learn more about how your faith developed and evolved. Please tell us about some of your earliest faith formation memories.*

100. Berni: I remember going to Mass. I had to have been five or younger. I was lying on the kneelers, bored out of my mind and watching the dust bunnies on people's shoes. I love that memory. I don't know why, but I do go to that. I also remember Latin was still part of the Mass, and that I didn't understand it or English. Spanish was my parents' first language, so the Latin was just another thing. But there was something so… I don't know. I just have that clear memory of lying on a kneeler.

101. Then, when I got my driver's license, I could go wherever I wanted to go; it was very liberating, because I could pull into my parish. That was a very big sense of independence and connectivity to the Lord. That is a good memory. I was sixteen by then.

102. Laurie: *What struck me is that your parish was a place you wanted to go. You must have already had a strong sense of connection with God at that point to desire to go there when you had your license. Where did that come from?*

103. Berni: Two things, one being named Bernarda but being called Bernadette until high school. Every year, when the film "The Song of

Bernadette" would come on, that was my film; that was mine. Clear the decks! I don't care what anyone else is watching. There will be a tantrum if I don't get to watch this movie! I would wait every year, looking at the TV guide, waiting for it to show up in the listing, circle it with a lot of pen, ballpoint pen, and then plant myself for the viewing. And yes, the world had to stop because I was going to watch this movie. My parents had a TV in their room; it was the second TV in the house. The ability to be in their room watching that movie and sitting on their bed was a huge privilege. My parents would allow me to do that, and to the degree that my brother and my sister wanted to roll in, that was fine. I'm the oldest. But I was going to watch this movie. So that was something I felt very connected to, and her story is so beautiful.

104. The other memory was from when I was very, very young; I think maybe five or six. I had a very high fever, and my parents were dabbing me with cold compresses. There was the sound of a humidifier going, and my parents left the room, but left a slight crack in the door for a little bit of light to come into the room. Against the light coming in the room, I remember there was the tiniest speck of dust floating in from the edge of my field of vision. As it floated down, I can't explain it well. I'll try. I had a sense of everything: I mean, like I knew that leaves were growing on the trees, I knew that there were millions of human beings and as if I knew each of them, like life was exploding and cells multiplying all around me. Everything was present to me in the moment, all of a sudden, everything was... micro-present but macro-existence. As this little speck of dust floated down, my focus was on that, yet I had this sense of the omnipotence, omniscience, omnipresence, omni, omni, omni. Just... there. And then, when the spec landed, it was over. That moment has also sustained me. It's been interesting because I've tried to re-capture it. I can recall it in a dim way but that electricity of a moment, I have never experienced again!

105. And I've had other beautiful moments, like in Eucharistic Adoration. It's so powerful. Don't you wonder, when the door closes, what's going on in there? Is nuclear fusion going on inside that eucharistic box? And then, when the door opens all of a sudden, or if you keep it open and the world is looking in - "Holy Spirit, everybody settle down!" But then, when the door closes, it's like - [Berni waves hands and makes party gestures and Laurie laughs.] You know, a lot

is going on in there! And so, Eucharistic Adoration becomes fun for me sometimes; imagination takes over and it makes me even laugh to think about what's going on in there. We don't get to see it, but someday we will. I mean, it is going on. It's just that we don't get to see it yet.

106. It allows me to go back to that moment, whatever it was, from when I was a child. I was so sick, but I knew about that speck of dust. Then, in prayer, how to focus on something that allows everything else to be there and present. That's the Communion of Saints. That is a reality that exists. I got a split-second taste of it somehow.

107. I've asked my parents, "Do you remember me being sick?" They say, "Yes, we remember you being sick, but we don't remember your epiphany moment. We don't, we don't, we don't." I said, "Did I talk about it?" "We don't remember." I think, "What is going on?" I so want them to remember something about it. But anyway, it was mine for the Lord to give to me, and it's constantly like the carrot dangling in front of me. "Go find it. Go find it. Go find it."

108. Those are three key memories I can point to: having my driver's license; a speck of dust; and then, just lying on and then falling off the kneeler onto the floor, with the dust bunnies and shoes and stuff with Latin going on in the background. Somehow, it was all very formative.

109. Laurie: *God works through all things, even the smallest things.*

110. Berni: Truly. Powerful memories!

111. Laurie: *When we talked before about Kairos versus Chronos, that showed me a great deal of depth in formation; that you've really delved into theology and are trying to understand your faith. How did that evolve? How did you gain that extra awareness and depth in your education about your faith?*

112. Berni: So, I don't consider myself well-read. I'm surrounded by people who are truly intellectuals. I've tried to read the summa, and I can't get through chapter two; I have to reread chapter one and two, and say, "Oh, for the love of Pete. I'm glad somebody knows this because it's not going into me!" But I've been involved in prayer groups. I have two different prayer groups that I've been a part of. I've also participated in *Endow Studies*. Much of my formation is just the layering of prayer with women of such deep faith and exploring and journeying together.

113. Then the other part is being in prayer. That gave me a lot of hope early on; maybe it made me lazy. But a lot of the saints weren't well-read. They didn't have access to beautiful libraries of books and things, but they did pray, and they did have the rosary. Think of the children at Fatima; even St. Bernadette was not considered cognitively brilliant. Other saints that make me want to be like them are St. John of the Cross and St. Terese of Avila. But then, St. Joan of Arc - what she had was courage and boldness. And I think, "Well, I don't, but I'm going to try!" Hopefully, when faced with those moments, I will have a whisper of her courage.

114. That has given me hope. I also listen to different podcasts. The world is filled; we have a two thousand plus year old tradition of content. Look at *EWTN* - I tune in to their different programs and what I love about *EWTN* is that it is efficient. Whatever program is on at that moment, if I turn it on, whatever I'm going to view, will contribute to my formation. It'll be efficient. I don't have to weed through chatter. They've done that. So, it has been a layering; I would say a layering as gifted by the Holy Spirit. It's grace. It's not the gift of intellectual rigor, although I keep trying.

115. Laurie: *Did you ever have any doubts about your faith? Did you have a "dark night of the soul" type of effect?*

116. Berni: Yes, there was a family tragedy. I had two aunts and my cousin's daughter (so a second cousin who was seven years old) that died in a house fire. That was a pretty brutal forty-eight hours, but by God's grace... The Lord only allows suffering for greater good. We don't know what that greater good is, but if I say, "Jesus, I trust in you," I have to believe. It is still hard to talk about. I will never understand. But my work is to continue to wrestle the emotion and make room for the hope and faith.

117. And then, gratitude. My family are all immigrants. I was born here in the States, but many of them were Cuban and literally floated across the ninety miles: you hear the stories, the sharks and all,

terrible, terrible stories. And so, gratitude that we had them for as long as we had them. Losing my seven-year-old niece - that was hard. (She was my cousin's daughter, but I called her my niece.) She was too young, but when faced with these kinds of monumental crosses to bear, I am flooded by God's grace. By God's grace, we have other family members here that we can lock arms with. By God's grace, gratitude for what we do have.

118. Trusting in God's Chronos, because we have Kairos. We don't live in Kairos, but we have Kairos because in the moment that the Lord was crucified, offered up His soul and descended into hell - in that moment - everything was there, past, present, and future. Again, I don't know who or when or what I heard that made that revelation so real to me and being able to live in that. Like this is chronological; this is the lightweight stuff. We do what we need to do because the Lord knows we can't handle Kairos. We can handle, kind of, Chronos. But that concept has been very - helpful - that's not a big enough word - it's been profound. It's been anchoring. It's been a big part of why I can trust.

119. When faced with humiliations for silly things that I do and other humiliations that come my way, I think, "Okay, Lord, fine! I really would rather not do it this way, but fine!" Just knowing that it is tiny, it's Chronos. It's just little crumbs along the way that are my crumbs. It gives me peace.

120. **Laurie:** *That is so insightful. It takes some of the stress off thinking that you have to do it all yourself, but it's also with an understanding of a greater and longer-term purpose.*

121. **Berni:** Yes!

122. **Laurie:** *Were there any other challenges that your faith helped you through?*

123. **Berni:** Divorce. I've been blessed in that divorce has not been part of my immediate family, but when friends go through it, it's very painful. So there I see the hubris, and it's more than concupiscence. It's that selfishness of original sin; that willingness to be alienated from God because of what I want.

124. In many ways, that is part of what prompts the work Rob and I want to do as it relates to K-12 education, because how do you help children develop a strength in their own virtues, in their ability to have a livelihood, help them understand the importance of leisure and that balance - all the different things? We're trying to shift into a very strong philanthropic mindset towards K–12. Nowadays, we don't even know what that word virtue means. And for kids, this whole idea of loneliness and how to make friends. How to endure. The devil is a liar - just fill yourself up with stuff for whatever pain you have.

125. [Going back to the story of the minivan, previously told with insights about being comfortable with myself and not bowing to what looks good, it is retold here with additional insights.] Remember I mentioned my mom's minivan that I owned twenty-five years ago? Well, I loved my van; the doors that open on the side and the captain seats. It was very cool. I loved that car. When the children grew up enough where I wasn't carting them around, my husband upgraded me to the fanciest SUVs - big, ridiculous. He loves cars, so he would buy me these big, beautiful cars. I should have been, and I was, grateful for the fancy SUVs. I had a BMW, and the BMW got bigger and bigger. I would say, "Okay, this is lovely, but I want a van," and he would say, "But you don't need a van," and I'm like, "Yes, yes, I know. But I **want** a van." And every year he said, "No, no, you don't **need** a van." So now I have two grandbabies, and I have a third one on the way. My parents are older, and we would like to ride in the car together to whatever mischief we're going to get into. So now, I want, **and** need, a minivan. Guess what? I just got my minivan! [She laughs] So I am now an official minivan-driving grandma.

126. The revelation was, the Lord knows. You pray for something you want, but it isn't what you need. But now my moment had come, I did need one, and the Lord answered my prayers in His good time. I'm a minivan Grandma! So, there you go. But it was funny, right? It's funny, because that is want versus need.

127. Laurie: *Answers to prayers! Speaking of that, what are some of your favorite prayers?*

128. Berni: "Jesus, I trust in you" is pretty much my go-to. I would say "Hail Mary" is a go-to in moments of joy, because of the beginning of it, "The Lord is with thee." The "Our Father" and the

"Glory Be" along with the "Hail Mary" - I mean the Trifecta - because they all answer everything! But, "Jesus, I trust in you" when I'm just under pressure and "Come, Holy Spirit" when I've been in situations where I'm going to be speaking on something; one never feels prepared enough. How could one possibly prepare for the privilege of speaking to a group on something? And so, I will begin with, "Come, Holy Spirit, whatever you want me to share here, help me to get it across because my life's experiences are only a result of something you want me to share with others." So those are Catholic go-to superpowers.

129. Laurie: *True, simple, but powerful.*

130. Berni: So powerful. They're succinct. They've got everything; they cover it.

131. I would say that in terms of saints, St. Terese of Lisieux is a favorite. I mentioned earlier that when I was on the last day of my agency on-payroll job, I was in New York and planned to show up for a celebrity-athlete filled pop-up party. It was 1997, the 100th anniversary of St. Therese of Lisieux's death, and there was an exhibit about her life at St. Patrick's Cathedral. I didn't know much about her, because in my family there were more "CEO Catholics" - Christmas and Easter Only, and the occasional Mass here and there; we'd go through spurts.

132. But this exhibit was just what I needed. I discovered, or rather the Lord introduced her to me: "I think you need to know the Little Flower now as you embark on full throttle, full face, frontal assault, motherhood. You should meet the Little Flower." So, He introduced me to her, and it has been a lifelong love with her since because she is so beautifully engaged in the smallest things being done in love for the Lord. You don't have to be other. You just have to be you. He created exactly as you are for Himself... to have that interaction with Him. So that was a gift. I'm so grateful to St. Patrick's Cathedral. Every time I go back there now, I again say prayers of gratitude. They have a beautiful little side altar there for her.

133. St. Joan of Arc is another key driver, "I am not afraid for God is with me. I was born for this." And St. Terese of Avila because she was so feisty and sassy and so brilliant. St. John of the Cross because he's

so deep, and he was good friends with St. Terese of Avila. St. Bernadette, for the reasons I mentioned previously, she's my childhood love and opened me to the reality of the communion of Saints! Padre Pio, because this was a man who was a holy man, and the beauty of his charism to purify souls through Confessions. There is a French poet who says that priests are the receptacles. But the word that he uses, or the way it's translated, is that they are the cesspools of society because they receive, and they're willing to hear and listen to all of our garbage and worse!

134. So it's also important to honor our priests and be mindful that they are set apart and chosen. How can I be, hopefully, a collaborator to the work that they've been called to do, and mindful that I've been called to work, too, in the vineyard? We work side by side. I was born post Vatican II, mindful that the clericalism of pre-Vatican II still exists. But know that I was born for such a time as this and to recognize how powerful the partnership is between our presbyterate and the laity, much like husband and wife, man and woman. The Lord gives us over and over so many examples where we can see how that collaboration just works, day and night. I can go on and on with these comparisons. It is so beautiful, so symmetrical. We have so little excuse to be afraid because it's all been laid out. It's like one ginormous safety net for us to do our best within it.

135. That doesn't mean we won't be afraid. Fear is a great prompt to get in gear and go deeper. But at the end of the day, what's the problem? Things are going to be great. I have this grace; I'm in the palm of his hand, protected and safe.

136. On those rare occasions that I feel like I'm being pushed out of the nest, it's because I'm being asked to grow. So those moments of suffering or humiliation or when things just happen, it's like, "Okay, Lord. Darn it. Really? Okay, fine. But."

137. Laurie: *[Jumping in with a similar thought]* - *"Thank you for that lesson, I think…"*

138. Berni: Yes! Exactly! "Can we just gloss over this one? I don't like the homework." It is like the Litany of Humility, right? Brutal, but it's so good.

139. All the litanies are so beautiful. It is a humiliation that I can't memorize them. There are people who know all the beautiful praises, the responses and when to shift gears. I need all my papers. I need all my little prayer helpers. I show up with my little stack. "How many years have you been at this?" "Well, I know, but I can't seem to memorize this." It's a humiliation, and as an example of the Lord's mercy to me, small in scope.

140. Laurie: *Thank you for your humility in sharing that with us. Trust me, many of us can relate! But you also give us courage to not let that stop us from growing and becoming part of the prayer community working in the vineyard!*

St. Bernadette Soubirous [1]

LITANY OF HUMILITY

O Jesus! meek and humble of heart, Hear me.

From the desire of being esteemed,

Deliver me, Jesus.

From the desire of being loved...

From the desire of being extolled ...

From the desire of being honored ...

From the desire of being praised ...

From the desire of being preferred to others...

From the desire of being consulted ...

From the desire of being approved ...

From the fear of being humiliated ...

From the fear of being despised...

From the fear of suffering rebukes ...

From the fear of being calumniated ...

From the fear of being forgotten ...

From the fear of being ridiculed ...

From the fear of being wronged ...

From the fear of being suspected ...

That others may be loved more than I,

Jesus, grant me the grace to desire it.

That others may be esteemed more than I ...

That, in the opinion of the world,
        others may increase and I may decrease ...

That others may be chosen and I set aside ...

That others may be praised and I unnoticed ...

That others may be preferred to me in everything...

That others may become holier than I,
        provided that I may become as holy as I should...

Part 3
Leadership

Leading in place is great, critical, I would say. A huge percentage of people lead where we are, but that other kind of leadership - to lead into the void - that's where I have experienced the most growth and the most grace, because that's where the Lord went, right into the void. (para. 161)

Success is knowing that you are loved and knowing that the gifts you've been imbued with are very particular and very important. How that shows up is being comfortable in your own skin that the Lord gave you - that's your wrapping, right? And you've got these gifts inside that are bubbling and bursting to get out. Share those gifts - share them! (para. 192)

---

141. Laurie: *Now we can shift to discussing leadership because you've bridged faith and leadership so beautifully by talking about the role of the laity and your passion for helping the youth. You've been involved in many different boards. How do you go about selecting which boards to be on, or to support?*

142. Berni: So early on, the Lord would put something in front of me that piqued my interest, and I would get involved. I would volunteer and I would get to know the organization better. I'd probably spend about a year volunteering. You get to know so much from the ground up. I learned a lot about good governance and poor governance the hard way because I was in the trenches.

143. Usually, all these organizations have a gala or fundraiser event, and I would invite Rob. I'd say, "Okay, Rob, I want you to learn more about this organization with me." Some we'd pass on, and I wouldn't get Rob involved. Rob was busy building the business, and I was busy learning about nonprofits. I would pull Rob in after a year or two. We usually didn't give much money; very, very little - intentionally so. I gave of my time, and I wanted to learn about the organization first.

Then, when Rob would come in, I'd say, "Well, what do you think?" And then he'd start to point out things about it. Sometimes I'd say, "Well, I disagree. I really like them," and Rob would say something like, "I think that leader is going to be difficult to transition from founder to scale," or whatever the issues were, but together we would do an assessment. If it was something that we both felt that we, as a couple, could get involved in more deeply, then if I was invited to be on a committee or a board, I would raise my hand and say, "Yes, Okay," and then I'd jump in.

144. Rob has his own methodology, but together, for the most part, we would compare notes and then go along. I got more and more involved, but I was mindful in identifying Catholic organizations. The key criteria was that it involved the Church.

145. One of my first roles as a board member was with the *Girl Scouts*. It was the Orange County Council, and I'm grateful for that experience and the people I met. I had been a Girl Scout, and I had benefitted from the organization. The national Girl Scout organization was going through some very big transitions during my board service. I learned a lot, and so it was fruitful. I learned I didn't want to be a part of an organization that was secular; it threw me deeply into the Catholic space.

146. Geographically, I looked at local, regional, national, and international nonprofits. On a horizontal plane, I looked at Catholic pillars: Catholic education, priestly formation and vocations, pro-life and so forth and then got involved. My involvement, whether on the board or as a volunteer, allowed me strategic and tactical awareness. "Oh, in the pro-life space: you have *Students for Life, Live Action, SBA*. This one for political, this one for advocacy…" I was very involved here at the local level, in clinics and pregnancy resource centers shifting to a medical model; I became friends with different people from the different dimensions of the pro-life movement and shared across segments what was transpiring.

147. For example, when I served on the board of *Obria Medical Clinics* here in Orange County, they were developing a national response to *Planned Parenthood* with a pro-life clinic network. Our Advisory Board was composed of the top leadership at key pro-life organizations, including an ecumenical outreach through groups like

Focus on the Family based in Denver. That included Michaelene Fredenburg of the *Institute of Reproductive Grief Care* who focused on miscarriage. It is rarely addressed. All the terrible but innocent things people say, trying but not addressing it, like "You'll have another one." But in many cases, that child is forgotten. And so, in conversation with all these different groups at this Advisory Board meeting, it was brought up that *Planned Parenthood* was trying to conflate miscarriage with an abortion, as if these were similar situations; that a woman's feelings were similar. It was useful for all the organizations to have this insight.

148. With our ability to have that conversation and drill down on that issue, we started to watch for what we are looking at in terms of legislation. The abortion pill wasn't full on; RU-486 [mifepristone primarily used for medical abortion] didn't have the momentum and the awareness yet. But as we started to see all these different pieces, we asked, "How is this medical culture or the secular culture, the pro-abortion culture, trying to stitch together this stuff to conflate the tragedy of an abortion and a different tragedy of miscarriage?" One, the mother chooses for the child to die. The other one is a natural result of that child's viability. So, because I was aware of various things, I was sought after for board positions in the pro-life space.

149. In the leadership space for priests, it was not dissimilar. I served on the board of *Catholic Leadership Institute*. I would be involved in those meetings, and I was aware, for example, that *Word on Fire* and Bishop Barron were developing something for priests. There was another group called at that time, *Leadership Roundtable*. I think they've changed their name, but I was aware of their curriculum. They had a pastor's toolkit that was a checklist. Also, *Amazing Parish* was targeting parish leadership and doing things. Again, because as a board member, I felt, and still feel, that it's my responsibility to be aware of the competitive set because that's what you do in the for-profit world. If you're selling *Nikes*, you need to know what *Adidas* and *Converse* are doing. So, if I'm trying to bring leadership to our priests and our clergy, I need to know what other people are doing in this space, and how they are doing it. What are we missing? What could we do better? Where could we collaborate so that we're not duplicating efforts? Where can we strengthen all these groups?

150. It's not about merging these groups and becoming the Ferris wheel of leadership for priests. The Holy Spirit gave me this analogy: "Why is it that in the Church we have thousands of hamster wheels to address homelessness, or whatever, when what we really need is the Mother of a Ferris wheel?" Right? But in order to build the Ferris wheel, and that's not to deprecate or to say that competition is not important, I think it's very important, because it keeps each of us sharp, but we need to do it with the beautiful Catholic idea of charity towards each other, and to make each other stronger.

151. It's not that I'm going to take market share. It's, "How can I make you better and you make me better?" But the other thing is, don't duplicate efforts. There will be some overlap, but a donor's gift is a widow's mite, and we need to treat that donation like a widow's mite, because it's given through the sweat of somebody's brow and through deep effort. The nonprofit community is, for the most part, very aware of how hard it is to receive a donation and then work three times as hard on how to use that resource and invest it to reach their mission, or to plow it into whatever their vision and mission are.

152. So again, because I've been in the midst of these different things, and because I looked at it vertically as well as horizontally - geographic and then the Catholic pillars, I just became the messenger of a lot of different, "Oh, and then they're doing this, and it's really great." Well, that's a trap door. Are we providing the kind of springboard to make sure that somebody can bridge right over that? I've been told that it was helpful that I could bring those kinds of insights.

153. Then the other side is confidentiality, because it's a privilege to serve on these boards; one needs to be hypersensitive to the confidentiality and what happens amongst this hand-chosen group of people to advance a mission. Rob and I get into this a lot because he's on boards and I'm on other boards. We have worked really hard to not have crosstalk, because even if it's committee work, I'm not on that committee, and I'm not on that board, so I shouldn't have the privilege of information unless I was voted to be on that board. That's why you have nominating and governance. That is very important. Be prayerful and use discernment about what could help these organizations.

154. The earlier example I gave you of the Advisory Board for *Obria Medical Clinics* was again super trench work, but also had these other groups involved at different levels. We had an incredibly well-informed group of people on the pro-life front. We didn't all agree, but there was enough respect in the room to say, "We have to put our cards on the table and compare notes because there are lives at stake. There are our own efficiencies, but we don't want to be duplicating. And we need to respect the donor widow's mite and how it's going to be used."

155. I've had ringside seats to great leaders. I've witnessed founders who've transitioned from founder to emeritus. I've seen that done well, and I've seen it done poorly. I've been involved with organizations that have been in existence for a long time, and transitioning wasn't the issue, but there were other issues.

156. I've watched organizations that got too burdened with what was fashionable. In this example, it was the whole idea of Spanish language materials. We know the demographics. Yes, it's true that the growth of the Spanish language audience in the Church is growing, and at the time it was very fashionable to make sure that all your materials were in Spanish as well. But I spoke up forcefully about how I didn't think it was a good use of our resources right then to develop Spanish language materials, because I felt that our target audience was, for the most part, bilingual. While they might be Spanish language dominant, there was enough of an English capability that it didn't merit using precious resources right then.

157. We had to decide on growing an audience, more deeply penetrating an audience or trying to capture this audience. The Spanish-speaking language skills in the United States are a wide spectrum, precisely because you have those who are not going to learn to speak English, and then you have those who are bilingual. You have those who are acculturated. You have those that are assimilated. It's a big moving target. So those are the kinds of conversations that are tough, but if I'm invited to be on a board or a committee, it's to be able to speak from the experience of my journey that the Lord has allowed me to travel through. And to speak it with charity and honesty and trust the other people on the board, because, like I said, in this case, I was the only person who felt that way.

158. It's hard to say, but I suspect my voice carried a different weight because I speak Spanish, and no one else did. I am Latina-ish because of my parents being immigrants. It's not a card to be played, but it is information to share with this nonprofit about how to think about and use your resources. In that case, what ended up happening was that the idea of developing Spanish language materials was tabled for about two years. I think the plan was for a year at the time, but it ended up being two years because they had to fundraise for it instead of using immediate funds. But in a leadership role, I want to have the ability to speak candidly and be comfortable in my own skin. I'm not there to make people like me. I'm there to speak from my life experience.

159. I am also involved with *Tepeyac Leadership Initiative (TLI)*. It is an organization that was founded in the Diocese of Phoenix by Bishop Olmsted and Cristofer Pereyra. It encourages the laity not by saying to them, "You need to get involved by working for the Church." They're not looking for more church business managers or parish managers. If there are some in the group, that's fine, but the focus is more to encourage confidence in where you are placed in your profession or your career; to be a Catholic presence in the world; to have the confidence to seek opportunities to serve on boards and to take on leadership positions.

160. I have the privilege of speaking on a panel at TLI's *The Hour of the Laity Conference* once a year. One of the things that one of the participants asked was, "Are there ever fights?" I think that's the word he used. "Do you ever get into fights on the board?" And I had to chuckle because I had never thought about it that way. Well, it's not like, you know, knuckles: Brass knuckles are not pulled out. Blood is not drawn. But absolutely, there are "difficult discussions", and in my opinion, if you go through a board meeting without having discomfort about some topic, then the board is not challenging itself and leading, because that's where the difficult conversations have to be held. When it trickles down into the staff and to the people who are on the front lines, hopefully, you as a board have thought about it, have noodled this, and thought about what the consequences are. That's where it is important.

161. So, I did share with them [the conference attendees], I said, "If you're on a board where it's kumbaya every time, and then you go

and wine-and-cheese it, think about if that's the kind of person you are. If yes, then good for you. But are you leading? Are you addressing issues? Are you the vanguard? Are you on the frontier? Leading in place is great, critical, I would say. A huge percentage of people lead where we are, but that other kind of leadership - to lead into the void - that's where I have experienced the most growth and the most grace, because that's where the Lord went, right into the void."

162. Laurie: *Where do you think we need that lay leadership the most right now? Where do you see the biggest challenges that are either in the Church or within society? We've touched on several of them, but just to encapsulate from an engagement perspective. If you are a lay person, and you're looking to make sure that you're doing your part in the best way possible, where are the biggest needs that you see?*

163. Berni: I would say truly, it is the partnership with the priest. How do you best support your parish? Support the priest; the priest is the leader. Again, if we look at Scripture, you know the husband, Christ [and the priest in persona Christi], and we are the Bride of Christ; we're the Body of Christ. So, from a subsidiarity level, it would be a relationship that I, as a lay person from the pew, can say to my pastor, "Where do you need help? What are we trying to accomplish here?" That is subsidiarity - that's our cell. That's our family, if you will, as we look at the Church. From a solidarity standpoint, all of those cells are working together; all those little parish families are working together to advance the mission. Let's say it was pro-life. If we at the parish level took up pro-life and if we gave our pastors the courage to speak up in the way that they know in their hearts what the truth is - and what's required of us to be courageous - that might abolish abortion.

164. Have you ever stood next to a pastor at the end of mass for a few minutes and just listened? I don't know if you have Laurie, but I encourage people to do that. Just stand to the side and listen to what people say. This is real. One time I was standing there, and I heard a person complain to the priest that there was a change in the toilet paper in the public restrooms. Really, do you think that this man… [Berni tosses her hands up.] Okay. Whatever. That was their

complaint. And then the other extreme was somebody who came up and gushed about the pastor's homily, as if it was the second coming!

165. So, this priest has these two extremes, and the people that come up to him to say things are frequently at opposite ends of the spectrum. The people who are putting their head down, raising their families, doing what they can to get through life - it's that bell curve - they are the bulk in the middle, but they are not the ones who pull the pastor's ears. So, what perspective does that pastor have about the world? You got the sensitive types that want better toilet paper - I was just so frustrated, I wanted to go and bop them on the side of the head. I was like - really? But then you have the other one, clericalism, that's ridiculously ingratiating and just too much.

166. So, to answer your question, we as laity, who are rolling up our sleeves and getting the work done, need to sidle up to our pastors and say, "We're here for you, and if you have a powerful homily on the challenges of same-sex attraction, or the horror of abortion that affects our friends, our sisters, our daughters, we stand with you. There are a lot of us, and let's have a bigger conversation." But we let our pastors go at it alone.

167. The pastor doesn't know who to call to say, "Let's have an invite for our parish family to get together to discuss this." It'll be difficult. There are professional moderators to walk through these things. So, I would say that's where it starts, but it also takes the pastor saying, "I need your help." And for the pastor to say it in a way to mobilize and organize these things. And it starts with small things, right?

168. Our Church does that, but I think evangelical churches, are far more welcoming or inviting. I don't attend those churches, so I don't know, but what I've heard is that they have lots of little jobs that people can accomplish and get them involved. "Show up because you're going to hand out roses for Mother's Day." "Are you picking them up?" "No, someone else is picking them up. But we need you to stand there and hand out one rose per mother. We need five bodies." Little things like that, whereas my observation is in the Catholic Church, it's the same ten people. It's the Parish Council that does everything, and we're not good at inviting others to help us carry the load. People will feel like they have purpose if they're a part of it, even if they are CEOs [Christmas Easter Only] and the only thing they

did for the year was, "I passed out flowers for Mother's Day." I was useful. I was important. But we're not mindful enough of that sort of invitation and the ability for people to do those things. And if you're afraid of the rejection, "No, why are you asking me that? I don't know you." Okay, you're an adult; that person is an adult, too. And if they say, "No, thank you. I can't." Fine. Move on to the next person.

169. In many ways, we're so tangled up in - I don't think it's being polite - I think it's more fear of rejection or being overly cautious. Yes, but you're there for the Lord! You're trying to invite people to the Mother of a Banquet that is happening every half an hour every day somewhere in the world. There is always the banquet being prepared and served. You're just inviting people to a massive party. What is your problem? If they don't want to come, fine, but you're not going to invite people? My goodness.

170. Laurie: *And then how do they take it from that parish engagement out into the secular world?*

171. Berni: So, I pretty much beelined from my *Girl Scout* board experience into my children's Catholic school, which then kept me in this beautiful bubble of this Catholic space. And so, I have not ventured out of serving within this Catholic space. Now some people might say, "Well, then, that's easy," and I would say to you, "Have you ever been involved in friendly fire?" In some ways, it's more painful because you're Catholic and I'm Catholic. I had a woman who was a friend that I loved and still love, who asked me to not interact with her any further because I was pro-life. We were both Catholic. She has a beautiful love of Our Lady. She's Catholic. She receives the sacraments. But we disagree on life, and she didn't want my emails; my approach was not one that she received well, and she asked me to stop reaching out to her.

172. So, to your question, one way that I can be a Catholic woman, present and export that is, I think, by wearing a crucifix. I've developed an allergy to gold chains, but I have little pins of different saints. So, I went into a very popular sandwich shop, and the young cashier said, "What's that? That is so cool." And I said, "Oh, it's a pin. It's a saint. I'm Catholic," I said. "It's a pin of a saint, and I wear this because I love thinking of this saint." It was St. Claire of Assisi. She said, "So what's her story?" I responded, "Well, she was a super-rich

---

girl, and she was beautiful, but she would watch this man who was St. Francis of Assisi. Do you know St. Francis of Assisi?" And she said, "No." I said, "Okay. Well, St. Francis of Assisi, was a poor, poor? Well, actually he was born wealthy, but gave up his wealth and became poor. Everything that he received he would give to the poor. And so, St. Claire saw what he was doing when she looked out of her fancy castle window, and she wanted to do the same thing. But this was a very long time ago, and women didn't do that. But anyway, they cut off her hair, and she DID do that. I love that story, and so I wear her pin." And so, the clerk said, "Oh, my gosh, that is so cool." I asked, "Are you going to be here tomorrow because I'll bring you a pin. I don't know if it's going to be St. Claire. Do you like Our Lady of Guadalupe?" "Who's that?" Well, then, the line's getting long behind us. People were like, "What is this? Just get the sandwich and go!" But that is just being who we are wherever we are.

173. I had a neighbor who bought her home and invited me to come see it. She was getting ready to remodel it, and she knew that I had been through a remodel, so she wanted to talk about that. I'm not sure how it came up, but I said, "Well, I'm Catholic," and then she said, "Well, I used to be Catholic. I'm a recovering Catholic." I said to her, "Oh, my gosh! That's a terrible affliction." I said, "Tell you what, come to my house. If you come to my house every day at three, we can do the Divine Mercy Chaplet, but if you come in the morning, we can say the rosary together. But if you want to start earlier than that, let's go to Mass," I said, "and then you'll get over that condition right away!" Okay, now her eyeballs became, you know, huge. I said it joyfully, because I meant it. She didn't know what to do with that, but I wanted to let her know that two doors down from her, there was somebody who felt that was not cool, not funny, but I wanted to do it in a way that was, I don't know - joyful, not judgmental, and with an open invitation. So, when she sees me on the street, she waves. She hasn't shown up at 3pm, and she hasn't shown up at the parish for Mass, but I keep praying for her.

174. So many different examples. We bought a home that had a ton of rose bushes on the front, and we pray the rosary in that house; it's a second home, and we've hosted events there. We have a statue of Our Lady inside. We had the house blessed, and this year, the roses on the front of the house are so magnificent that you don't believe they are real. It's so breathtaking. A number of the neighbors, when

we pull up to the house, have said, "We just want you to know that the family that put those rose bushes in eight years ago never had roses like that." They could see that we never changed out the rose bushes. Somebody said to Rob, "We don't know what you're doing, but we need your secret." And Rob said, "Well, I can tell you what it is. We pray the rosary, and it's Our Lady. She loves roses." We just have to speak plainly. This is our daily life. This is who we are. It's Our Lady if you want to know what the secret is. It's not Miracle-Gro. It's Our Lady's rosary!

175. How to be a layperson in the world is to be a Catholic who is joyful and proud of it. Just be so filled that you are given the ability to share the overflow. I'm grateful that, by God's grace, I have received the gift and opened the box. I just want others who are holding the box to open it up. I want to say, "Pull the bow off. What are you doing? You've got the gift in your hand! Come ON!"

176. Laurie: *I think that sounds beautiful, particularly with children in mind. They say that the mood in the home comes a large part from the mother, and the father as well, but particularly the mother. Can you touch a little bit on that and what faith and leadership look like within the family?*

177. Berni: First, I'm going to go to Rob, because my grandbaby girls like to see Rob with the rosary beads in his pocket. I also try to wear clothes with pockets, and I always have a rosary in my pocket, and if not, then in my purse. I want the girls every time they touch me to know that's what's there and to reach into my pocket and pull that out. Now, they're two and four, and they don't pray the rosary, but they know Grandpa Rob has one, too. So, there is this sense of that is something special. It might be for adults, but even now they have their own rosaries. But that's an example.

178. When we go to Mass, we genuflect before we enter the pew and depending on where the Eucharist and the tabernacle are, we turn. My granddaughter said, "How come you turn?" I said, "Well, Jesus is in the tabernacle over there. It's not just forward. It's where Jesus is." Children like those details. They want to be a part of it because they want to do it right. And those are also like a secret code. "Oh, you turn this way. Oh, where is it?" So, they've got to go find it; it's like

"Where's Waldo?" "Where's the tabernacle? Where's Jesus?" So that is beautiful and fun for children. They're not too little.

179. Another thing, my daughter has brought in whenever we're driving: If we pass church, make the sign of the cross, because our Lord is there. When we hear a siren, the girls will ask (they call me Gigi), "Gigi, let's pray." That's what they say! "Let's pray!" And I'll say a prayer for whatever that siren is for; that's a cry for help. We come up with scenarios of what it might be. It might be a mom who's pregnant, and she's got to get to the hospital quickly. It might be something sad, and we go through some different scenarios because you want them to know that life is a myriad of things, and that a cry for help can be for something joyful as well as for something sad. But Jesus is always in the midst, and you always make the sign of the cross to seal it. They don't quite have the order of how to make the sign of the cross, and their hand goes around, you know, [Berni gestures] but they know there is something going on with their hand. It's supposed to be up there, which is just so beautiful to watch.

180. Laurie: *Since we are talking about leadership in helping to develop spirituality in others, especially within the family, can you talk about experiences that particularly impacted your family, such as your trip to Europe?*

181. Berni: In January of 1997, I knew that I was leaving my job. (That was the story of my last night in New York City, and the Lord introducing me to the Little Flower.) I started planning an extended trip to Europe. So, I got home from that NYC trip, packed in forty-eight hours, and we got on the plane; it was the four of us, my husband Rob, me, and the two children who at the time were in second and fourth grade. My son had done his First Communion two weekends before, and I had requested through the diocese tickets for an audience with the Holy Father, Pope John Paul II.

182. And so off we went, and the mindset was twofold: One Europe, because I wanted to visit other countries besides Spain and I wanted the children to experience something other than the U.S. And two, my son had just received First Communion, and I wanted him to have the experience of Communion at any place in Europe, and my daughter as well. She was two years ahead in her Communion.

51

183. I planned a two-month trip; Rob could only stay for the first two weeks. He jokes that he had to come back home to finance the rest of the operation, the three Neal assault on Europe. I gave each child a whistle, and I had a whistle, and I said, "Stay close." We didn't have cellphones then. I said, "If something happens, you grab that whistle and you blow hard. But whatever you do, run into a Church, and you'll be safe; you tell the priest or the adults there, if there is a problem, and what's going on." They carried in their pocket the card with the phone number of the hotel. Again, we didn't have cellphones, but a parish was a place where they would be safe. There were even more Churches than Starbucks back then.

184. So, there was a real sense that wherever we went, we were going to be just fine. We went from church to church. We fed pigeons. We saw beautiful art and architecture. The streets are imbued with a reverence, and an uplifting sense of what man is capable of and of beauty. You know there is a real sense in Europe of the importance of beauty, but beauty at the service of God, beauty to bring and draw others, and to offer appreciation and thanks. So, it was beautiful.

185. When Rob left, I thought, "Oh, my gosh!" Two weeks went by fast, and I still had a month and a half to go alone, responsible for Kira and Collin. I was also very aware that I didn't know how to be a mom day in, day out, and this was going to be my boot camp. The three of us were going to bond. I didn't think that I had a poor relationship with my children, but I didn't have the kind of relationship that I wanted because I had been traveling so much as a career mom. I did say to them, "Look, the three of us are on equal footing here. The only difference between us is that I have a driver's license and a credit card, but other than that, we're on equal footing. So, I expect you guys to pull your weight in this exploration of France, Italy, and Spain."

186. So, we would hit the postcard rack when we got to a new city. Then they'd each pick their ten things that were intriguing to them; then we'd go on a scavenger hunt to find those things. We would spend about five to seven days per city. There were days that they were just sick of moving from museum to museum to Churches to historical something, which was fine. Some days we just sat on Church steps, fed pigeons and had a baguette with cheese for lunch.

It was magnificent, and my children remember so much of it, even though they were so young. Again, they were going into third and fifth grade. It made them aware of the world in a whole different dimension.

187. It made me aware of how important this kind of leisure is, because we were absorbing - we were just drinking from the stones of the buildings and the thousands of hours and years that those church places and church sanctuaries were there - all those prayers. It's all there. So, we were there just inhaling, and they can tell you very powerfully in their own words. When I asked them, they said, "Oh, Mom, it was a great trip. Really bold!" They can't believe we did that looking back, but they're so glad that we did.

188. But it was even more profound after that first experience of seeing Pope John Paul II drive by in his pope mobile. Several years later we had an opportunity to meet Pope Benedict XVI, and both my children, now in college, came to that meeting. It was so beautiful because they both said, "Pope Benedict XVI took your hand. You didn't shake his hand. He took your hand, and he looked into your eyes in a way that made you feel like he was saying, 'Oh, my goodness! I lived my whole life to meet you.' You just felt like you looked into his eyes, and there was eternity. There it was." There was Kairos, and he was just so present. My children are the ones who phrased it that way and have gifted me with that phrasing for it. They expressed "He was just forever. He was just there for you. He made it seem like meeting you was the most important thing he could be doing in that moment." Pretty profound and what a gift!

189. And it was only a few seconds. You're in a line, and then it's over. Those seconds were a privilege for my children because they had a chance to feel that and say that... How rare! How profound! And then to try to be that for others; we can't touch it, but we try.

190. Laurie: *That's beautiful. As you were talking about it, I was remembering that little speck, that focus, and that sense of "omni, omni, omni" that you had as a child; it seems to all come together with what you were just talking about. That is beautiful.*

191. So, we as Catholics don't necessarily define success the way that the world defines success. Can you talk a little bit about that? That'll be our wrap-up. It's all about life, faith and leadership - in that aspect - what is success?

192. Berni: Success: Success is knowing that you are loved and knowing that the gifts you've been imbued with are very particular and very important. How that shows up is being comfortable in your own skin that the Lord gave you - that's your wrapping, right? And you've got these gifts inside that are bubbling and bursting to get out. Share those gifts - share them! Do not get bogged down with, "Oh, I can only...," or "Yeah, I'm a terrible cook," or "I'm not a good writer," or "I'm not an intellectual," - whatever those things are - do not get bogged down in that!

193. Success is saying, "These are my gifts." Think of the Little Flower and say, "My tiny little gifts, but I put them at the service of the Lord." And hopefully, I'm comfortable with who I am and its littleness - that it's the other person who's big, right? Because they probably are big. They're usually amazing. And if you're able to connect in such a way that they feel like, "Oh, I want to share my gifts with you, little as you are..." "Sure! Fine!" Right? That's success. That's relationship, and you can only have relationship "with two eyeballs at a time," to borrow from one of my back in the day advertising terms. You can only click with that person who's seeing that commercial - "two eyeballs at a time." (Even if it's the Super Bowl ad, and millions of people are watching it!) So, when I'm standing in front of somebody, and I'm the Berni Neal commercial, my hope is that I'm successful and I capture those two eyeballs that are tied to a heart in that moment, and I'm able to have that person feel like they can share with me, "Tell me, I want to know!"

194. So, my question to you, Laurie, have you ever met somebody that when they tell you their story, you don't say, "Oh, you should write a book," or "That could be a feature film; that really should be a feature film."

195. Laurie: *Every time I do.*

196. Berni: Every time.

197. So, every time, can we get that person to share that story? This is a quotation I do want to share with you from Henry David Thoreau; I've been told that he's not accurately quoted, but it's the way I heard it, and it's the way I say it, and it's what grips me:

"Men lead quiet lives of desperation and go to their graves with a song in their heart."[2]

198. I heard that probably in Junior High, and it gripped me. Frankly, it made me angry because my Catholicity tells me - not on my watch, not on my watch! I want to hear that song. For everyone I meet, I pray, "You will not go to your grave without singing."

199. Laurie: *That is inspiring!*

200. Berni: And that is success.

---

[2] The first half of this quotation is from Thoreau's *Walden*:
"The mass of men lead lives of quiet desperation."
The second half may be from Oliver Wendell Holmes' (1809-1894) "The Voiceless": *Alas for those that never sing, But die with all their music in them.* https://www.walden.org/what-we-do/library/thoreau

The Power of Philanthropy
Berni Neal

The Hour of the Laity Conference, TLI Inc.
November 8, 2024
Christ Cathedral, Orange County, CA

201. Monica Hannan Introduction: As a marketing expert, Bernie Neal is well-aware of the fundraising challenges in Catholic education and nonprofits, and she applies her skills to promote the works of the Church and Catholic organizations. We are glad she does.

202. She serves on the governing boards of *EWTN, Legatas, Live Action* and *Thomas Aquinas College.* She has also served on boards or committees for *Catholic Leadership Institute, Magnificat Foundation, Given, World Priest, Woodson Center of Free Speech, Civil Rights Coalition,* and *Vanguard University Committee* to eradicate human trafficking.

203. Please join me in welcoming Bernie Neal who's going to speak on *The Power of Philanthropy.*

204. Berni: Good afternoon. So good to be here with all of you. All of you spell hope, power, potential. First, I want to thank Cristopher and the Tepeyac Leadership Initiative team; even preparation for this was just phenomenal. I've had the chance to speak at other events, and I just have to say the TLI team is really formidable. So, thank you, Cristopher and the team.

205. Thank you to Bishop Olmsted who responded to the call, much like Mother Angelica. For those of you who are familiar with the story of Mother Angelica and *EWTN*, the Holy Spirit spoke, and Bishop Olmsted, like Mother Angelica, responded. This Tepeyac Leadership Initiative speaks into a vacuum that used to be there, but now hosts not only conferences like this, but I look at the graduates and the people that I've been able to participate with on a panel, and truly, this is where The Hour of the Laity and the future of the Church resides. So thank you for being here.

206. I was born to immigrant parents and grew up very happily about seven miles away from here in what was then a solidly middle-class white community. I'm hoping that this is far enough away from my hometown that I'm avoiding Jesus's admonition that no prophet is accepted in his hometown. I'm no prophet, but this is my hometown.

207. We were an immigrant family where Spanish was the dominant language. Spanish? Yes, Spanish. My dad is Cuban Korean, and my mother is Dominican Chinese. It makes for a fabulous Thanksgiving meal of gratitude.

208. My parents modeled giving in a very personal way, the daily grind way, a bed to anyone in need, a meal accompaniment, hospitality for immigrant families that arrived from Cuba with absolutely nothing. My childhood home was their first stop. For many individuals who wanted to learn and attend college in the United States from the Dominican Republic, our home was their first stop. I shared my room and my closet with many a girl trying to dress the part for their new life here in the United States.

209. Then in college, the Lord saw fit to introduce me to a wonderful, fascinating man, Rob Neal, but this young man was on the other end of the California spectrum. He was a fourth-generation Californian. He's a big shot now - Chair of the *Catholic University of America*. He was the one charged by then Bishop Todd Brown to take this campus from Dutch Reformed with Reverend Schuler to the Catholic campus that it is today, and I'm very, very proud of him.

210. When we met, he had only ever traveled away from the beaches of Southern California to Hawaii. By dating me, he was able to experience a version of Asia, Latin America, and the Caribbean without ever pulling out a passport. Forty years later - we've been married for forty years - forty years of hard work later, and the blessing of financial success, we are discerning how to give it away; how to invest it for returns that elevate humanity and bring as many souls as possible into the Sacred Heart of Jesus.

211. I like to describe our home as a lay Catholic economy. Rob earns it, and I give it away. That's not totally true because he's very much a part of the benefaction planning, but it doesn't make for as good a soundbite. But the point of fact is, it really is harder to give it away

than it is to earn it. To earn it, you have to put your head down and get to the task at hand. To give it away, you have to look up and observe this huge landscape of need and then choose a path knowing that even the recipient carries a burden. This is a simplistic comparison, but you often hear about the misery of a lottery winner who is suddenly rich beyond their wildest dreams and quickly comes to grips with the burden of wealth. On the flip side, the Holy Spirit keeps apostolates on financial fumes, lean and hungry, so that we don't become fat and sassy. This way, the donor and the recipient become partners, married to the mission, and committed to the outcome and the offspring.

212. So why give it away? Once the basic necessities of food, shelter, and clothing are covered, why not spend the remaining balance on ourselves? Get stuff, get more fancy stuff, more, more. If we were like St. Francis of Assisi, the amount for the basic necessities would be part of the philanthropic calculation. It would be giving away all, all, all - the shirt off our backs. But if a person gives away everything, does he still have power? Did St. Francis of Assisi have power?

213. There is an inherent sense that wealth equals power. What is this kind of power? This power is transactional. Yes, of course, one can buy many things, but does it buy the one thing that men seek? Paraphrasing GK Chesterton, "Every knock on a brothel door is a search for God." It is a search for love. A new friend just shared this with me, and it's burrowed into my prayer time: "The very finest things in life God gives us for free, but we're determined, determined to buy the second best, the counterfeit, and those things are very expensive."

214. Why is that? The World Giving Index says that how an individual perceives their current life situation is linked to their likelihood to donate money. In other words, happy people share. Let me read that again. How an individual perceives their current life situation is linked to their likelihood to donate money. In Aristotle's Nicomachean Ethics, he says in essence, "Happiness is the one thing you can choose for itself. Everything else is selected for the sake of happiness." That means that happiness is at the root of every decision and action we make. It determines whether we think our lives have meaning and whether we think life is worth living.

215. We've all been living with something in the air that feels a little sadder, a little meaner, and a lot less hopeful. In fact, in 2022, the year-over-year charitable giving dropped for only the fourth time in four decades. The amount of giving has grown since then, but fewer people are participating. In 2023, *USA Giving* stated that the number of givers in America plummeted from two-thirds twenty years ago to just under fifty percent. Can we make the correlation that fewer people are happy, and consequently, fewer are giving?

216. The work of charity is frequently defined as providing immediate relief from suffering: providing meals for the homeless, and medical support for victims of a natural disaster. This would be defined as the work of charity. Whereas philanthropy is described as seeking to transform and not just treat. It looks to address root causes.

217. There are voices that criticize philanthropy as fundamentally flawed. Why should individuals have this power when the government can do it? They argue for wealth that is more equitably distributed and governments with progressive tax systems. Here's an example of government distribution in action. On May 13th in 2022, California Governor Newsom announced a $100 billion surplus. On March 26th, 2024, twenty-two months later, California announced it was facing a $73 billion deficit. Did Californians experience a better quality of life from the $100 billion tax boom, tax dollar surplus? Many of you here are probably Californians, you can answer that! California burned through $100 billion in twenty-two months. Imagine what might have been had private hands been able to respond and develop more imaginative, nimble philanthropy versus handing it over to the California state government.

218. For comparison's sake, the Vatican's total wealth is estimated to range between ten and fifteen billion dollars. So, when you hear people say, "Well, the Vatican should just sell everything they have, and we would be able to solve world hunger." There you have it. Our Church at its very core is ordered to the complementarity of solidarity and subsidiarity.

219. What the secularists cannot stomach is that philanthropy frequently steps in when government fails. Even more telling is that Church philanthropy is made up of faithful in every tax bracket who respond to the call with the formidable trifecta of time, treasure, and

talent. Imagine our Church with $100 billion! A philanthropic power to uplift those in need, and our assistance would go far beyond California borders. Our Church goes out to the margins: a parish church in every corner of the world, a priest offering the sacraments, the reality of Christ present everywhere. This is the power of the Church. This is the power of Catholic philanthropy: presence, subsidiarity, those of us who use our hands and feet to be the voice of our Lord in every tax bracket. This must make the bureaucrats tremble.

220. Recall, the widow's mite; she gave not of her surplus, but from her poverty. She offered her whole livelihood, two small coins. It was generosity and the courage of conviction. Ladies and gentlemen, as Catholics, we have conviction in spades: we believe, we know, we consume the body of Christ. John 6:55 "For my flesh is real food and my blood is real drink."(NIV) And ten verses later, we hear that from this time many of His disciples turned back and no longer followed Him. We have conviction, and we have the source of eternal life. The amount of money is just a measure. It is not about how much you give. It's about the heart of why you give. The widow was a philanthropist, and her might, M-I-G-H-T, was foundational.

221. So here we are, fall of 2024 and President Trump has won the election. The citizens of the United States of America have voted overwhelmingly for a country where equality of opportunity, a level playing field for everyone, is the bedrock of how to lift up our country. It is a core American principle. The majority of American voters said the solution is not to pull down and to force equality of outcomes. We have ability, brain and brawn. We have faith in ourselves and in our neighbors.

222. Opportunity is back with a vengeance, and the timing could not be better for Rob and me. Here's why. The summer of 2022, Rob woke up and said to me, "We need to be more strategic," and I thought I was being strategic!

223. It made me really think about how did we make our decisions for those first ten years as a young family, and how did it differ from the way we were making them now? How were we learning about organizations? Well, quite honestly, those first few years we started by volunteering for things that our children chose, and that's how we

found out about different things. We were both working parents, but we were very determined.

224. Rob has great memories of his painfully shy mother overcoming that to be his Cub Scout leader. My mom was co-chair of my grammar school Ways and Means Committee. (That's what they used to call Advancement and Development - Ways and Means. I think we should bring that back!) She was chair of that committee a mere fourteen years after first stetting foot on American soil. I remember working together with my mom on the Oktoberfest with my dad, my brother, and my little sister (I think she was still in diapers). I remember that feeling. It gave us something to work for together that aspired to something beyond ourselves. I wanted this for myself and for my children.

225. What had I done in those years before Rob woke up and said, "We need to be more strategic." I had mapped out a grid and I thought it was a pretty good plan; I was really proud of it. I thought about the context of local, regional, national and global and then I layered the Catholic context, pro-life, education, marriage, social issues, evangelization, media, vocations, and religious life.

226. We watched the work of organizations like the *Ethics and Public Policy Center*, *Communio* that focuses on marriage, *FOCUS* on missionaries, *Patients' Rights* that looks at euthanasia, *Students for Life* with chapters in every college if possible. *The Beckett Fund*, and *Religious Freedom*. Locally, I was involved in *Obria* pro-life clinics, regionally *Thomas Aquinas College* (although we now have a campus in Boston), nationally. *Legatas, Live Action, Pueri Cantores Liturgical Choir* music for children, *Catholic Leadership Institute*, global *EWTN*, *The Papal Foundation and The Magnificat* - how many of you are subscribers? Thank you! We were invited to serve on committees for some of these groups and in some cases, we were invited to serve on their boards. This gave me a front row seat to decision making at these apostolates as well as interfacing with some of the most incredible thought leaders, intellectuals and doers of our Church.

227. We started investing and partnering with organizations to think into the future, and to take risks. This is a difficult thing for us. We are so cautious; we need to take risks. Did you know that the dominant personality profile of most priests and religious is

introverted and non-confrontational? We said to the priests, "You are not alone. We walk with you. We're a team, collar and necktie." But what were we really accomplishing for all of this involvement? Those words kept just beating in my head. "We need to be more strategic."

228. We spent the rest of the summer talking about it, and Rob highlighted two key factors: capital allocation and long-term patient investing. He felt these were the two key factors for his business success, and we wanted our role as philanthropists to have these characteristics.

229. We wanted to look at philanthropy as capital allocation. We wanted to be a force multiplier, piggybacking on what exists and not building a vanity plate for ourselves. We wanted to go upstream. What problems are seemingly intractable? We wanted to be strategic in identifying our mission and not necessarily our passion. It had to be grounded; grounded in a Catholic philosophy and anthropology in truth. It would get at the deeper root causes of whatever issue we discerned.

230. That fall providentially, Rob sat next to Dr. Andrew Bella, who you'll hear from later this afternoon. He's the dean of the *Bush School of Business at Catholic University of America*, and Dr. Bella told Rob that this was incredibly innovative thinking. So we met with Dr. Bella and began to tease out a plan, but here was our fear. Would we choose the right issue? This was a moonshot. Would we put our ladder up against the right wall? We wanted to make sure that our investment was inherently valuable and provided the power of philanthropy to drive transformational change even if we did not choose the right wall. Could our efforts strengthen marriage and families, and foster a culture of virtue?

231. So we made a list of the people to speak to. We thought we needed to interview as many people as we could. Our strategic goal is to have a significant impact in one or more of our targeted areas, but we needed their involvement. We called this the vision discernment process. Here's what we asked. We ended up interviewing almost thirty-five different people from across the spectrum.

232. We asked:

- What do you believe are the most pressing issues facing the US right now?

- In any of these issues, do you think we have hit or are about to hit rock bottom?

- What issues will become pressing over the next twenty years that aren't getting enough attention right now?

- Which issue would you recommend that we address, and how would you go about addressing it?

233. We are now in phase two and that is to articulate in as much detail as possible the nature of change that we want to drive over a twenty-year period. Long patient investing.

234. This is our mission statement: promote marriage and family, faith and virtue, through K-12 education and associated programs. We are putting the power of philanthropy behind K-12 education. We hope for transformational change that will help children become lifetime learners, not lifetime workers.

235. The third step for us will be to gather the best social science - **science** - which means scientifically rigorous and grounded in an authentic anthropology. There is a lot of social science out there that has led us astray as a society. If it's not actually Catholic, it must at least be consistent with a Catholic view and not opposed to it.

236. Next, we want to map out a series of strategic steps to determine what our intermediate goals are. These will be leading indicators that will help guide us in understanding if in fact we are on the right path. Then we need to develop measurement tools. Longitudinal studies are not exciting. They're hard, and they take commitment, but it's important because we're in this for the long haul. And then, the real work of the foundation can begin. We are now deep in this because the train has left the station. So here we come to a key point for us, the power of philanthropy.

237. The real power of philanthropy is our understanding that it is stewardship. God is the owner; man is the manager. We are but stewards in collaboration with God. Rob and I are only on this journey with God's grace. Nature becomes super nature when it is charged with God's grace. God gives us wheat; we make bread. The Lord takes this bread, and the physical matter of the bread is changed into the physical matter of Jesus's body and gives us eternal life. Jesus says, "Whoever eats this bread will live forever." (John 6:58) God also gave us free will. We can choose the path of salvation or not. We are invited to join God in his eternal redemptive movement.

238. Are Rob and I motivated to do good because we will look good? This will certainly make us feel good and quite happy, but this is a slippery slope. We win no matter what we do here because giving philanthropically is perceived as an honorable, moral and a selfless act, and it is. But we have to soul search what is being asked of us, even if it will make us happy. Is this work worthy of the distinction as collaborators with God?

239. Here is what my experience thus far has shown me. It is in partnership with the Church that we're able to provide charity, philanthropy and add the critical dimension of stewardship. This is the power of philanthropy. This speaks to the thriving of the human person on a temporal plane and on a spiritual plane. It is collaboration with God, with priests, bishops and cardinals, and with those individuals who are willing to lead, like all of you here and those who are inspired to work alongside us. It is because we are made in the image of God. We are challenged to go out, and in the words of St. John of the Cross, "To put love where there is no love and there you will find love."[3] It is the desire for the individual, the family, and the community to pursue happiness through their own agency.

240. Those with no religious affiliation, the nones, N-O-N-E-S, are rising. The number of priests, bishops and cardinals reaching retirement age is also rising. We are living during a dramatic shift in

---

[3] *Letter 26 to Madre María de la Encarnación in Segovia (excerpt)* Written from Madrid 6 July 1591;
https://carmelitequotes.blog/2022/07/05/juan-ltrs25-26/

society. A 2017 study (I'm sorry I couldn't find something more recent) by the Pew Research Center is important to bring up here. They noted that the current models of parish life cannot be sustained when the number of churchgoers in their fifties and sixties declines by 8.3 million people and the resources decline by almost five billion dollars. We will have less money and less people to do more work. We are living in a change of age, and the Lord made each of us precisely for such a time as this. Let our Catholic numbers rise to meet this challenge; we must get creative. We must be willing to take risks and trust in the Lord. We must ask Our Lady to help us meet the challenges that we face today.

241. Loneliness is the one that baffles me the most. How can this be? How can this be loneliness? Paraphrasing Henry David Thoreau, "Men lead quiet lives of desperation and go to their graves with their song in their hearts." Not if we can help it! We are cavalry! We Catholics are determined to hear every song of every single soul.

242. It is up to us. "I'm not afraid... I was born to do this," said Joan of Arc. We are One, Holy, Catholic, and Apostolic Church. Perfect truth handed down through the most imperfect means. I give thanks to God that He has seen fit to invite me to be a collaborator in His work. My consolation: God does not call the equipped. He equips the called to work for the salvation of others, and in His mercy, those souls are impacting my efforts at my own salvation.

243. French Catholic novelist Leon Bloy said, "The only real sadness, the only real failure and the only great tragedy in life is not to become a saint." (from La Femme Pauvre) I leave you with these thoughts from Lumen Gentium, our guiding star for this conference. "It is the love of God and the love of one's neighbor which points out the true disciple of Christ." "They must devote themselves with all their being to the glory of God and the service of their neighbor." (para. 42,40)

244. We are here. We have the heart, the passion, the resources, be it the widow's mite or a donation with many zeroes. We have the grace, so let's get to it. The power of philanthropy is in this room. Pope St. John Paul II said, "The future starts today, not tomorrow."

APPENDIX II

God's Call, A Woman's Response

Berni Neal's Nuggets of Success & Stewardship

"Like good stewards of the manifold grace of God, serve one another with whatever gift each of you has received." (1 Peter 4:10)

245. This appendix is a collection of Berni Neal's guiding principles, faith insights, and service philosophy ~ a resource for readers to turn to for distilled wisdom and guidance in discerning where God calls the heart.

246. The selections were curated from Berni's personal notes and a series of talks she has given in her philanthropic work. They supplement her story and provide inspiration for how one can integrate the Catholic faith into both daily life and professional vocation.

Life and Feminine Genius

From a speech given at Our Lady of Mount Carmel Church, Balboa Island, CA, February 1, 2018

247. The woman finds in each life something unrepeatable, something wondrous.

248. One could argue that it is the unchecked compassionate, sensitive nature of a woman that has evolved to being permissive of all forms of behavior. We have no guardrails. No tolerance for painful discussions, pain or suffering.

249. But I believe that women steeped in faith are imbued with a wisdom regarding pain and suffering.

250. Motherhood (parenthood) means joys and sacrifices. From the moment of birth, the sleepless nights, the financial sacrifices, the personal sacrifices because the child was more important. The

future was more important than ourselves. Self-giving feeds the hope and potency of the future. Look at the role and impact on society of many saints: Think of St. Katherine Drexel, St. Elizabeth Ann Seton; Servant of God Dorothy Day; St. Mother Theresa…

251.   The prophets promised a Messiah that would free the Jews; they expected a military response to free them from Roman rule. Our Lord came alright: with weapons to fight against money, power, pride. His weapons were poverty, humility, and obedience. So we should not be surprised if our neighbors find our faith bizarre, offensive, or even intolerable. It places pressure on our resistance to sensibilities grounded in original sin… Thank you Adam & Eve.

252.   From the very first chapter of the Bible, in Genesis we are taught that women, like men, bear the stamp of God's own image - men and women were created equal.

253.   If you read Genesis carefully, we have no basis to assume that Adam was in any way lonely or that he felt any insufficiency. Adam lived in a perfect world and had perfect communion with God. I suspect he did not feel any sense of loneliness. Adam did not need Eve to fill an emptiness in his life, he needed a wife to fulfill his God-given mandate. Woman was not created to fill a social or sexual need in Adam, but to complete the Lord's purpose for humans. Eve was not needed to complete Adam, but to complete God's command to Adam.

254.   A woman's capacity for generosity is tied intimately to her receptive nature. Direct Proportion. Give/ Get.

255.   The first generous act is to welcome new life, and in this, Mary is our best example.

256. There are many Gospel accounts of generous women.

   o The widow's mite reminds contemporary women that the size of our offering is less important than the orientation of our hearts.

   o The woman who anointed Jesus with the precious perfume teaches us to recognize human value over material value.

   o The generous hospitality of Martha and Mary and their warmth of service and friendship.

257. Jesus trusted women's generous hearts with his own human need for hospitality, support, and understanding of his mission.

258. The Church perceives the grave danger of today's propaganda. Secular society is pulling women away from this generous nature. It encourages a selfish language that is allowing women to "regret" their children, "regret" their marriages - never mind that many have successfully combined "success" with virtuous lives and hypocritically raise up those women when it suits them.

259. That natural generosity is a weapon against dehumanizing scientism. Women emphasize the social and ethical dimensions to balance the scientific and technological achievements of mankind.

260. We were made for this time by God to give our unique gift to the world; but we were also made in this time of the world to help receive the gift of salvation.

Faith and Purpose

From a speech given at Catholic Charities Ventura, April 2017

261. If, science is study of facts - then, how does science explain love? How does science account for that transcendent spark that connects two people?

262. True love as being self-sacrificial rather than self-seeking.

263. In conversations: do we try to find common ground vs. mentally preparing an argument to enlighten them on the error of their logic? This would be classified as tightrope conversations. Fight the urge to have the last word.

264. We all want: Respect | We don't want: Contempt

265. It's been said that sports chat rooms are one of the few places we can find civil dialogue. Apparently since these fans, while strangers, share loyalty to a sports team, it allows for common ground and enough respect to hear another point of view. They are bridge conversations.

266. How can we build upon our shared values with the 'nones,' family members, etc. - like the sport chat rooms, to build bridges within our community?

Catholic Leadership and Service

From a talk given at Legatus Pittsburgh on the Feast of St. Peter Damian, 2019

267. Leadership is the art of motivating a group of people to act towards achieving a common goal. BUT Catholic Leadership is mindful of the people's gifts. Motivate them to act towards achieving a common good.

268. Why is it such a battle to serve?

- o Confuse complaining with solving.

- o Change is difficult. It's easier to just do the same thing.

- o People forgive sin but not arrogance.

- o Weak leaders surround themselves with even weaker people.

269. But SERVE we must. We are called to help others meet Christ through lives of Holiness.

270. The Church pushes back on the culture: to serve, to defend the unborn, the oppressed, the depressed, distressed. The Lord has a plan. Did Adam and Eve's disobedience make us potentially stronger? Does this allow us to face our cross in a way that the Garden of Eden masked our potential?

271. We like to congregate with like-minded people but are there areas in our life where we allow ourselves to be challenged? In many instances it is our very children that exasperate us and maybe that's precisely God's plan.

272. I will Bless the Lord at all times. We are doing it right if everyone is feeling a little challenged. (Pushing the boundaries.) Christ did not set us up for comfort but for glory.

273. Christ suffered on the Via Dolorosa. It is difficult to serve because God let's suffering happen to bring about the greater good. It is precisely what we should be doing. The more we encounter these difficulties the more surely we know we are in alignment with His will. Before Easter Sunday is Good Friday.

274. Catholic leadership builds upon the desire to promote the welfare of others: philanthropy.

275. We don't come to worship to get anything. We do get something, but that's not why you come. You come to give yourself over to the work of the philanthropy of God, bringing to completion the salvation of Jesus Christ.

"For where your treasure is, there your heart will be also."
(Matthew 6:21)

Quotations and Scripture: Writing on the Walls

April, 2021

During a home remodeling project, favorite quotes, prayer cards and religious medals were incorporated into the very walls of Berni and Rob's home, like a hidden time capsule of grace and blessings.

Den

- *I am, you are not.* - St. Catherine of Siena
- *Do Whatever He Tells You.* - John 2:5
- *The only real sadness, the only real failure, the only great tragedy in life, is not to become a saint.* - Léon Bloy

Den Wall to Dock

- *Above the clouds the sky is always blue.* - St. Therese of Lisieux

Living Room/Den Shared Wall

- *In one kiss, you'll know all I haven't said.* - Pablo Neruda

Living Room to Dock

- *He who sings prays twice.* - St. Augustine

Living Room

- *There's only one way to experience an abiding peace that transcends circumstances - by faith.* - Evers family member
- *A world at prayer is a world at peace.* - Fr. Patrick Peyton
- Mother Mary prayer card

Kitchen

- *If every tiny flower wanted to be a rose, spring would lose its loveliness.* - St. Therese of Lisieux
- *Whose hands are God's hands but our hands?* - St. Therese of Lisieux
- *Make sure that every person of whatever background can find in you a welcoming heart.* - Pope Benedict XVI

Dining Room

- *Truth is not determined by a majority vote.* - Pope Benedict XVI
- *Let science tell us what and how. Let religion tell us who and why.* – Pope St. John Paul II
- *The cross reminds us that there is no true love without suffering, there is no gift of life without pain.*
  ~ Pope Benedict XVI

Entry Lights Switch

- *Each of us is the result of a thought of God. Each of us is willed. Each of us is loved. Each of us is necessary.* ~
  ~ Pope Benedict XVI.

Entry Hallway

- *If I could tell you what it meant, there would be no point in dancing it.* - Isadora Duncan
- *Every part of the journey is of importance to the whole.*
  ~ St. Teresa of Avila

Garage Hallway

- *The future starts today, not tomorrow.* – Pope St. John Paul II

Bottom of Stairs - Hallway

- *Trust God that you are exactly where you are meant to be.*
  ~ St. Theresa of Avila

Twin Bed Bathroom

- *The darker the night, the brighter the stars. The deeper the grief, the closer is God!* - Fyodor Dostoevsky

Craft-room Bathroom

- *Love is an irresistible desire to be irresistibly desired.*
  ~ Mark Twain

Master Bath Vanity

- *I am not afraid; I was born to do this.* - Joan of Arc

Master Bedroom

- *For when I am weak, then I am strong.* - 2 Corinthians 12:10
- *It is only with the heart that one can see rightly; what is essential is invisible to the eye.* - Antoine de Saint-Exupery

Bedroom(s)

- *The Lord will fight for you, you only need to be still.* - Exodus 14:14
- *It was too easy to die for what was good or beautiful, for home or children or a civilization - it needed a God to die for the half-hearted and the corrupt.* - Graham Greene, <u>The Power and the Glory</u>
- *Hate is a lack of imagination.* - Graham Greene, <u>The Power and the Glory</u>
- *Let us forget with generosity those who cannot love us.* - Pablo Neruda
- *Put love where there is no love and there you will find love.* - St. John of the Cross
- *If he asks much of you it is because he knows you can give much.* – Pope St. John Paul II

TLI

We hope you enjoyed this book.

Please consider supporting our efforts by learning about,
praying for, or financially supporting
Tepeyac Leadership, Inc.

Please visit:

TLIprogram.org
THLconference.org